LIKE NO OTHER *school year*

Pamela (Livingston) Gaudet

2020, COVID-19 AND THE
GROWTH OF ONLINE LEARNING

Like No Other School Year:
2020, COVID-19 and the Growth of Online Learning
(Livingston) Gaudet, Pamela

ISBN 978-1-7357474-1-5

© 2020 Pamela (Livingston) Gaudet. All rights reserved.

Contents

ABOUT THE AUTHOR 5

Chapter 1 – Introduction 7

Chapter 2 – Learnings 15

Chapter 3 – Social-Emotional Health & Learning 43

Chapter 4 – Leadership 69

Chapter 5 – Relationships 81

Chapter 6 – Communication 97

Chapter 7 – Online Learning and Teachers 109

Chapter 8 – Cybersecurity and Technology 137

Chapter 9 – Summary and Recommendations 149

Chapter 10 – Interviews 161

The Interview Questions 219

Bibliography 221

ABOUT THE AUTHOR

Pamela (Livingston) Gaudet has spent most of her career in K-12, initially as a teacher and later as director of technology for public, independent (private), and charter schools. Pamela joined K-12 education after the birth of her daughter, seeking a more compatible schedule as a parent.

At The Fieldston School, her first K-12 position, she asked teachers if she could sit in the back of their classrooms while they taught. Most said yes. She observed firsthand the art and skill of teaching and the generosity and collegiality of teachers. Working at Fieldston inspired her to take on director of technology roles at schools in New York, Pennsylvania, and New Jersey.

Pamela then moved to develop software that teachers would use in the classroom. She held roles in product management at Tutor.com, Schoolwires/Blackboard, Age of Learning, and SungardK12/PowerSchool. In late 2019, Pamela left PowerSchool to consult and write full-time.

Pamela holds a BS in computer systems from CUNY/Baruch in New York City and an MS in education and technology from Chestnut Hill College in Philadelphia.

The author of two editions of the ISTE book, "1-to-1 Learning: Laptop Programs That Work", Pamela has written for educational magazines and journals.

Pamela is happy to speak with you at pamelagaudet@productvaluesolutions.com or http://www.productvaluesolutions.com.

Acknowledgments

This book happened because of the generosity and kindness of over three dozen educations, with thirty-two interviews appearing in this book. Contributors have kindly written chapters and pieces for the book, including Michelle Back, Susan Davis, Mike Daugherty, Ethan Delavan, Lindy Hockenbary, Christina Lewellen, Scott McLeod, and Adrian Segar. Kymberli Mulford helped with early organizing and editing. Betsy Palmerston did final edits. Adriana Tavares created the beautiful book cover. Alex Inman, Joel Hames, Lisa Nielsen and Sarah Hanawald provided advice and feedback.

Dedication

This book is dedicated to my two favorite and most-loved people in the world, my husband Brian Gaudet, and my kid Bryce Livingston. Brian is my best friend, counselor, advocate and daily inspiration. Bryce is a talented writer, a kind friend to many, a hard worker and an all-around mensch. How blessed am I.

Chapter 1 – Introduction

A World Upside-Down

Everything changed. All around the world. Nearly all at once. A deadly virus plunged us into grief, fear, and anxiety. And schools had to continue, somehow. Educators had to find a way to do what they do best – take children from wherever they were, to a better place. The educators stepped up.

Educators Shared

Thirty-two educators told their stories and shared recommendations for this book during live recorded video sessions one-on-one conducted by the author. Questions were open-ended and are included after Chapter 10.

Public, independent (private), and Catholic school educators were represented. Educators were interviewed from both rural and urban schools, and schools with a high percentage of children who qualified for the school lunch program.

School leaders/educators were chosen from the author's Professional Learning Network (PLN) and by referral. Six educators and four contributors wrote insightful pieces.

The original research was included from the interviews, from a survey of teachers by Daniel Cruz and Megan Storey Hallam, and podcast interviews by Dr. Scott McLeod.

We Were Still Hurting

The pain continued. We were still living in a world upside-down with grief from the loss of normalcy and lives lost. Schools grappled with whether to open or not, and what open even meant.

How This Book Can Help

Learning from educators who have gone through crises can help prepare us for the next crisis, and for everyday life. How did educators cope, what do they wish they could have done differently? Did hindsight uncover gaps? Was this a time to think hard about what school means? What needs do teachers have in a new, online world? What permanent shifts in schools will come about following this worldwide experiment in online learning? These and other questions are addressed.

What You'll Learn

The commonality of educators from public, independent, Catholic, and international schools was fascinating. You'll learn what these educators said was essential, what they wished they'd had in place but was missing, and how they addressed issues around social-emotional health, equity, communication, and more.

Educators wrote chapters and contributions. An expert on Social-Emotional Health examined current programs and how they can help schools. A renowned professor who studies leadership in schools shared insight from his *Coronavirus Chronicles* podcast and a leadership seminar he ran. A tech director/author explained the elements of excellent communication during a crisis or anytime. A professional development expert shared aspects of online learning and described synchronous and asynchronous learning. Two experts at an organization for tech directors laid out the importance of cybersecurity with examples and links to help schools ensure they're ready for online learning. A consultant who conducts dozens of Zoom sessions monthly gave some tips. A parent with two school-age children talked about how they coped. Other chapters delved into relationships, shared the interviews, and tied things together with a summary and recommendation.

What You Can Take Away

School leaders all around the world are grappling with what comes next after a worldwide pandemic. How will schools operate, what is the value of school, how will instruction happen? Plans are being written and rewritten. Schools are opening and then closing mere days later when more virus cases turn up.

You will learn from the educators who went through this crisis., They will discuss what they feel was important in the moment, and what they anticipate should happen as a roadmap for the future.

Each chapter adds to the elements school leaders will want in their repertoire to help teaching and learning post-pandemic.

Readers will understand online learning, social-emotional health, communication, and relationships and design their plans to include these elements.

Your Author/Guide

I've spent my career in K-12, first as a teacher/tech director, then as a director of product management, developing software for schools. These roles were at public, independent (private) and charter schools. My daughter attended the schools where I worked until she was in 7th grade when she said, *"Mom, I don't want to be a faculty kid anymore. You know too much."*

My passion is around helping teachers. I believe that technology, used wisely, can help teachers reach students.

I believe that students should have agency and be stewards of their learning.

Two editions of my previous book authored as Pamela Livingston, "1-to-1 Learning: Laptop Programs That Work," were published by the International Society of Technology Educators, ISTE. For that book, I interviewed educators and shared resources from managing a 1-to-1 laptop program at a school. After writing that book, I helped schools in the U.S. and internationally.

When COVID-19 struck, I had just left my former software company employer and begun to consult. It seemed time to write again, hear educator stories, ask knowledgeable colleagues to write chapters, and to publish a book about this extraordinary time in the hope it could be a resource for educators.

What This Book Is/What This Book Is Not

This book is for school leaders, technology directors, superintendents, principals, and others in leadership positions at K-12 schools. It is not a book specifically for teachers. It is about systems and plans that leaders will want to have in place to address the shifting nature of schools in light of the pandemic and growing use of online learning.

A Few Assumptions

For consistency, the word school is used throughout the book, not school or district.

You will note that interviewees all had positions of leadership, yet not all were actively teaching. All interviewees are called educators in this book to acknowledge the heart of their words and work.

Lastly, 1-to-1 is mentioned several times. It means one device per student for learning. 1-to-1 became the operant term for giving students a dedicated device in the early 2000s when I wrote my book about laptops in schools. Since then, a significant number of schools and districts provide devices to children. It's this author's opinion that 1-to-1 should be the norm in every school and district.

▶ Like No Other School Year – Recommended School Leader Use of this Book

Arguably none of the leaders at your school has before undergone several months like what happened from March 2020 to the start of the 2020-2021 School Year. It's been like no other school year.

Ideally, there will be a leadership committee at your school to debrief, examine efforts, understand implications, survey your stakeholders, and make sense out of what happened when the school closed suddenly for the pandemic.

From that understanding, improvements and innovations can follow.

- ▶ Note the caret symbol to the left of this sentence. Throughout the book, at the end of each chapter, there will be **School Leadership Committee Takeaways** and questions from the chapter. This symbol highlights post-emergency learning lessons to consider for your school or district.
- ▶ Every school will be different, every lesson learned will vary, and the way forward will change according to the mission, philosophy, and needs of your school. Knowing some of the touchpoints to include in your evaluation, based on other educators' advice, will help you ground your efforts based on this research.
- ▶ As you consider members who will be on the leadership committee to debrief, analyze and make recommendations post-school closing, ask yourselves how you will involve your school's largest stakeholders in terms of numbers and sheer impact on their future lives: students.
  - ○ Students can be talented at planning, analysis, and making recommendations. They are inherently honest and straightforward. Consider giving students agency by putting them on your committee.

Note that Chapter 9 contains Essential Questions that your Leadership Committee can adapt to your school and district to survey your internal and external stakeholders. These questions are also marked with the caret symbol.

What's Next

Chapter 2 outlines the dozen learnings from the interviews. Interviews were analyzed and coded to identify themes described most frequently by educators during the interviews; a frequent mention of a theme became a learning. The rest of the book fleshes out these learnings, either throughout the book or with in-depth chapters.

Chapter 3 is written by Ethan Delavan and describes the importance of Social-Emotional Health and Social-Emotional Learning (SEL). Mr. Delavan expertly details the need for SEL in schools and recommends several possible programs you may wish to adopt.

In **Chapter 4**, Dr. Scott McLeod synthesizes leadership through the lens of a pandemic. His insights, based on his *Coronavirus Chronicles* podcast and a course he taught on leading through a crisis, are not to be missed.

The importance of relationships, including quotes and recommendations, is covered in **Chapter 5**. Interviewees highlighted the need for forming and solidifying relationships between teacher and student and teacher and parent, especially during a pandemic that closed schools. A first-person contribution by Michelle Back shares what her life with two school-age children was like during the pandemic.

Mike Daugherty, a director of technology in Ohio, takes us through communication in **Chapter 6**, and why it is essential to effective crisis management. Mr. Daugherty shares why good communication is the glue that holds schools together during crises.

Chapter 7 synthesizes an excellent eBook written by chapter author Lindy Hockenbary and includes research from Daniel Cruz and Megan Storey Hallam conducted with teachers about online learning; it also has useful Zoom advice from Adrian Segar.

Chapter 8, expertly written by Susan Davis and Christina Lewellen from the Association of Technology Leaders in Independent Schools (ATLIS), takes us through cybersecurity and the privacy policies and procedures schools will want to have in place.

Summary and Recommendations are in **Chapter 9**, including what schools will want to know and understand from the COVID-19 in order to move forward.

Chapter 10 has synthesized interviews from all thirty-two educators categorized by Public, Independent (Private), and Catholic schools. Their stories from the front lines told with grace and love will remind many of us why we are educators.

Chapter 2 – Learnings

Introduction

While COVID-19 was raging around the world claiming lives, I interviewed educators in school leadership positions. Each shared their struggles, successes, plans, and recommendations. I interviewed educators from public, independent, international, and Catholic schools. These educators spoke live through video calls from the U.S., Canada, Japan, Taiwan, and Turkey. Remarkably, even with the distance and difference in the type of schools, commonality existed. Arguably this was the most extraordinary time of their educational careers. Except for the interviewee in Taiwan, every school other closed during COVID-19. All thirty-two educators were on the front line during our conversation, supporting teachers, parents, and students through this unusual experiment of conducting online teaching during a pandemic.

The essential learnings are organized so the reader may delve into most of the topics with the chapters that follow. Recommendations support each learning.

- Most learnings have chapters (shown in parentheses) for more information:
- Social-Emotional Health and Learning (Chapter 3)
- Leadership (Chapter 4)
- Relationships (Chapter 5)
- Communication (Chapter 6)
- Online Learning/Teachers Stepped Up (Chapter 7)

- Tech Departments/Cybersecurity (Chapter 8)
- Infrastructure (Chapter 8)

The learnings with threads throughout the book are:
- Digital Equity/Food Insecurity
- Parents Gaining New Respect for Teachers
- Schedules Needing to Change
- Students' Resilience

The synthesized educator interviews are in Chapter 9.

Note: throughout the book, the phrase 1-to-1 has been used to refer to one child having one computing device.

Social Emotional Health (also see Chapter 3)

Everyday life changed completely because of the pandemic. Everyone struggled. Suddenly no one was going to school or work, or doing sports or any of their other usual activities. People experienced grief over their lost routines and sadness for the lives lost and illness around them. So much was gone, and so much was different. Struggles with this sudden change led to social-emotional health issues at every age level, in every socioeconomic group. Ensuring that all the stakeholders in the community felt supported emotionally and socially was a prime focus for the thirty-two people interviewed for this book. They shared their concerns for social-emotional health during this time of crisis.

All the Love That's There

Rural Payson, Arizona is a town with many farmers. Students who stayed home had to work the fields and help the business of their parents—the farm. Sometimes they had to leave the farm equipment idle to participate in synchronous online learning. The social-emotional health of everyone at

Payson was tantamount for Ms. Andrews. But students were coping with this unusual type of instruction.

"All the love that's there. Amazing for some classes – even high school – you'd think they wouldn't make as much of an effort. But they are there. Maybe they're working on the back field with a bulldozer but stopping to get on a video call."

> *Victoria Andrews*
> *Director of Technology and Innovation*
> *Payson Unified School District, Payson AZ*

"Lakota Local School District teachers came up with fun ways to keep students engaged and try to keep student spirits up. Everyone at the same time was home, and everything at home was different. The entire world around us changed so quickly. Norms and routines were gone. Teachers worked hard to involve students in fun activities and to reach out as much as possible."

"Our teachers have organized several activities and projects that support social-emotional health, community outreach and even a district-wide spirit wear week. Our teachers are very focused on developing the whole child—remote or not—and our teachers, staff, and especially students continue to overcome the barriers and rise to the challenge. And we all continue to learn a lot together along the way."

> *Todd Wesley*
> *Chief Technology Officer*
> *Lakota Local School District, Liberty/West Chester Townships OH*

Making Sure the Kids and Their Families are Okay

Administrators at schools started by making sure everyone was coping with the shock and change resulting from the sudden closing of schools all around the world. This kind of change, without notice, can cause disorientation and anxiety.

The educators I interviewed agreed on one thing: This was NOT the time for new learning; rather, it was the time to support students and teachers, and, if possible, to reinforce what knowledge already existed. Now was not the time to tackle brand-new concepts. Instead, the priorities were keeping up with students, ensuring that the connection to teachers didn't fray, and reaching out as much as possible to students, families, and teachers.

"We want to make sure kids are okay, and families are okay. We meant to provide students with support through this time. The Ministry said the priority is emotional, psychological support. To hell with marks, make sure the kids are ok. We had no expectation for students to do anything."

> *Jeff Whipple*
> *Digital Learning Lead*
> *Anglophone School District–West, Fredericton, New Brunswick, Canada*

Reduce Anxiety

Adults who had lived through many changes in their lives, both negative and positive, needed to let everyone know that "Eventually this too shall pass." It was difficult for students to understand this, and it was frustrating for teachers to have all their tools and effective techniques unavailable. Reducing anxiety and taking the long view helped. Some recommendations follow and are also contained in Chapter 3, Social-Emotional Health.

"Students and teachers need to know adaptability and reduce anxiety as it comes up in a normal process. Don't rush. All of us do too much. Just relax, it will be fine. Relax."

> *Vincent Jansen*
> *Director of Technology*
> *Southpointe Academy, Tsawwassen, British Columbia, Canada*

No Separation of Home and School Life

Before the coronavirus, students and teachers had time in school and time at home. The activities and the physical surroundings were different. It took time to get to school and then time to get home after school. Routines were in place. In school, there was before school time, perhaps homeroom, then classroom time. Depending on the grade level, students stayed in one classroom during the entire school day or moved to other classes. Expectations were different in school than at home.

During COVID-19 and school closings, there was no longer school life, just home life.

"The lack of separate home life and school life ... We cannot now separate this. The pandemic was an emergency situation--not planned online learning. We explained to teachers that it is not online learning. It's emergency online learning."

> *Burcu Aybat*
> *Primary and Middle School Principal*
> *Ielev School, Istanbul, Turkey*

Recommendations:

Social-emotional health was a consistent central theme from the interviews. Teachers, students, parents, and administrators all struggled with uncertainty, change, and fear. Nearly overnight, everything upended.

Schools should regularly conduct surveys, have "healthy time" drop-ins, ask all stakeholders what is needed, and find ways to make phone calls and face-to-face contact. Human-to-human interaction, even if only via screens, is vital during any emergency. Planning contact with families will be time and money well spent. The emotional health of your community members is worth it. Read Chapter 3 for more recommendations on social-emotional health from author Ethan Delavan.

Active, Caring Leadership – (also see Chapter 4)

Interviewees for this book were school leaders, either as directors of technology or with roles of school or district influence. Most were on the leadership team for their school or district. Every interviewee was actively leading their organizations and the school community.

 Effective leadership under pressure is an essential way of calming and righting a community.

"Our superintendent ran a meeting that kicked off with a song that represented a time he was emotional, and his wife put her head on his shoulder. That image will be framed in our minds forever."

> *Arline Pique*
> *Director of Technology*
> *Hamilton County Educational Service Center, Cincinnati OH*

"I think the way our Upper School and Middle School heads have handled the process of moving online might be a model on how to do it. They modified schedules and went right into formal training while being very supportive, doing what needed to be done to support faculty."

> *James Huffaker*
> *Director of Technology*
> *The Hun School, Princeton NJ*

Recommendations:

Strong leadership during a time of crisis is crucial for a community. Leaders connected to the school community understand what teachers, parents and students are going through. They must communicate with empathy and understanding to help a school or district during a crisis. Tone, message, and authenticity all need to be conveyed by leaders. It can be one of the most critical factors in determining how a community gets through a crisis.

Communication and Community (also see Chapter 6)

During and after this crisis, communication became vital to informing and calming the community going through the crisis. Active, frequent, and even-handed communication helped schools as they weathered the storm. Community members were in the loop when leaders shared what was coming, and when. The districts that communicated frequently showed respect for all their teachers, parents, students, and staff.

Keeping Everyone Informed

Making sure everyone knew what was happening even as school closing details shifted was essential to schools everywhere. Parents and students had to understand what to expect, and teachers had to prepare a new way of delivering instruction.

Educators interviewed described their approaches to communication.

Ms. Aybat recommended, "We needed to have one channel where parents can get true information. We created a good communication channel. Communication is so important. Not quantity, but quality was important."- Burcu Aybat

"(We worked hard) to help the community stay in touch. The American School in Bombay set up regular online parent cafés for elementary, middle, and high school. ASB also set up a single landing page for communication and video tutorials on their EdTech channel for virtual learning."

> *Mario Fishery*
> *Director of Technology Support*
> *American School of Bombay, Mumbai, India*

Community Coming Together

Many schools saw everyone in their community rise to the challenge, not just stakeholders. This emergency impacted people everywhere in some way. For some, it meant helping to supply Personal Protective Equipment (PPE) as this was in short supply during the pandemic. The community came forward to help.

"Foodservice workers gave their PPE to hospitals, so we used social media to say 'food service and custodial staff don't have any masks – is there anyone who can help?' Response from the community was overwhelming. The biggest success story was the community."

> *MaryEllen Bunton*
> *Director of Curriculum*
> *Danville District 118, Danville IL*

Students understood what the school community meant more deeply.

"These students will realize that community is more than physical. Being together is one sort of community, but an emotional community coming together does not have to be face-to-face."

> *Jason Kern*
> *Assistant Head of School for Innovation and Learning*
> *All Saints Episcopal School, Tyler TX*

One district in Pennsylvania appointed Jeanne Knouse, Director of Student Services, to coordinate their pandemic response. Ms. Knouse oversaw counselors, school nurses, family outreach, registration processes, All-Hazards planning, and ESL. She quickly looked at budgets and considered how not just the students but the families in the community could be helped. Many parents had lost their jobs, so they had no income. Food, rent, and necessities were at risk. Ms. Knouse reached out to the school community to ask for donations to the mental health budget she'd been putting aside for the next school year.

She thought maybe she'd get $10,000 or so. She was overwhelmed by the generosity of the community.

"Parents surprised us. They came up with $106,000! We distributed this by need for families in the community. Anything we said we needed, families came up with. One woman thought kids should have sidewalk chalk. We found a source and added it to their lunch bags. Another woman mobilized others and set a goal to make over 8000 (she is at 2000 now) masks for our students."

Jeanne Knouse
Director of Student Services
State College Area School District, State College PA

Recommendations:

The pandemic sent communities reeling. Everyone wanted to know the extent of the crisis, how it would impact them, and what they should do. A communication plan should be part of every school's Crisis Plan. Without effective communication that informs the whole community, morale will suffer, and people may veer off in unhelpful directions.

Communication is key to the success of what is coming next. Confusing, unclear, or contradictory messages can undermine the direction a school wants to take. Uncertainty can breed fear and doubt. When people don't know what is happening, they may imagine the worst.

Leaders and teachers should be able to amplify and support the communication from the school—provided they understand it themselves.

Schools may find their communities ready and willing to provide resources, help, and donations. A school is much more than buildings; it is also people who come together during a crisis. Many people saw the caring side of their communities during the pandemic.

Teachers Stepped Up to Teach Online (also see Chapter 7)

There was no interview question asking if teachers rose to the challenge of having to instruct remotely on a few days' notice. Yet nearly all of the educators interviewed described how teachers stepped up during this emergency in multiple ways. Every educator conveyed respect and admiration towards their faculty. Teachers adapted to previously unheard-of conditions, and they did it nearly overnight.

For teachers, this meant the disruption of instructional norms, challenges to existing schedules, and modification of instructional techniques. They learned new tools, collaborated with other teachers, addressed content differently, and rethought classroom management. Teachers figured out new ways to engage with students remotely. Technology moved front and center for reaching and teaching students. Even schools that had never mandated technology tools changed their expectations for teachers. Mastery of technology tools became a requirement.

New Expectation for Teachers to Use Technology Tools

Pre-pandemic, many schools selected classroom technology software but often did not require its use. Schools required their teachers to use some technology products such as the SIS (Student Information System) for student records, report cards, and discipline. Special education tools were also required.

Other products, however, such as the LMS (Learning Management System) were not mandated, so not all teachers used these tools. That changed once schools closed. Teachers had to give assignments and assess work. The LMS is a system used to manage assignments and assessment tools, so it became mandatory. Schools told teachers they had to learn the LMS and provided ad hoc professional development. Teachers needed to learn to use these tools so that students could access lessons and homework, and teachers could grade their work.

Schools set up professional development classes for the LMS, video conferencing tools, and other products. Drop-in sessions for teachers to ask technical and curricular questions became available nearly overnight.

Teachers had to accept the need and step up.

"...everyone has to learn how to use tools. Even if it's not their cup of tea, they understand the need." – Victoria Andrews

"Our elementary teachers weren't using the LMS before this and never had a vision of how to use it .... They didn't complain and have been so creative and found exciting ways to connect to kids."

> *Jennifer Fry*
> *Chief Technology Officer*
> *Delaware City Schools, Delaware OH*

Teachers Stepped Up to New roles – Needed New Support

Teachers sometimes found themselves becoming the front-line support with students' technology use. Teachers reached out to students and helped technology work at their own homes as well as at students' homes. In many cases, it was the only way to engage directly with most students who had the devices and the online access required.

Suddenly teachers found themselves answering student and parent technology questions that were previously handled by the school or district's tech support team. As the closest contact with students who were using new devices and tools, teachers did their best to answer student questions and refer to the tech department as needed.

It wasn't what teachers signed up for, but they helped out anyway.

Mashpee District gave teachers a drop-in support time they called "tech therapy" to support teachers who were supporting students and parents:

"Teachers had to step up, technology-wise. They became troubleshooters, tech support for their families. I'm really proud of teachers."

> *Suzy Brooks*
> *Director of Instructional Technology*
> *Mashpee Public Schools, Mashpee MA*
> *President of Massachusetts ASCD Affiliate*
> *Co-Author of My Modern Mentor, Lead Forward Series, Times 10 Publications*

Teachers Used Zoom, Microsoft Teams, Google Meet for Classrooms

Video conferencing became a critical tool. Schools made sure most teachers and students had access to video conferencing for synchronous real-time learning. Observation had always been a prime assessment technique for teachers, and it was challenging to assess via observation when students were not physically present. Teachers were forced to become creative about how to engage, motivate, and assess students.

> *"None of the teachers knew Zoom before this. They had to step up and learn how to manage."*
> *Darryl Loy*
> *Director of Modern Learning*
> *Good Shepherd Episcopal School, Dallas TX*

Teachers and the Vision for Teaching with Technology

Technology personnel in schools have been trying for decades to help teachers see the wisdom in using technology for teaching and learning. It has been a tough sell up till now. No longer.

○ **Author Anecdote**

I spent my career in schools persuading teachers to incorporate meaningful technology into their instruction. I developed a coffee addiction at one school where the only place teachers could congregate was during brief moments in the teacher's lounge, grabbing coffee. In one room, teachers got hot coffee, powdered creamer, sugar, and a word with the director of technology. Sometimes this type of persuasion worked, sometimes not.

Emergencies change things.

Although an ever-increasing group of educators saw technology as a way to accomplish educational goals, many busy teachers with full plates didn't immediately see how technology could enhance instruction and deliver outcomes. Almost overnight, a real-life example of how to reach students with technology presented itself. Many teachers saw the possibilities, sometimes for the first time, and grasped the vision. Technology was no longer an add-on or an "if you have time" activity for instruction. If you wanted to maintain your relationships with students, technology was key.

"We are seeing some great success stories with teachers. They are understanding how to make the shift, really doing a good job. They are really recognizing how to use tools asynchronously. "

> *William Fritz*
> *Director of Technology*
> *Sycamore Community Schools, Cincinnati OH*
> *Executive Director of Learn21*

"I'm constantly amazed at how faculty pivoted and adapted… to ask the whole community to switch to virtual school mode. Both asynchronous and synchronous – it's a big shift."

James Bologna
Director of Technology, Co-Director of Teaching & Learning
Global Academy Site Director
Windward School, Los Angeles CA

While not a cure for all educational ills, the meaningful use of technology to achieve deep learning goals presented itself to many educators. Some saw its value for the first time. Still, there was much more to accomplish. Embracing the idea was only the beginning.

Praise for Teachers Collaborating During Emergency Learning

Teachers didn't just learn new tools; they learned new ways to collaborate and rethink instruction through online learning. Educators interviewed shared how teachers reached out and worked with others and strengthened their Professional Learning Networks (PLNs.) Professional Learning Networks are comprised of educators who share, learn, and collaborate to help one another improve professionally.

In a typical school day in a physical school, it was hard to grab the time to collaborate with other teachers. Some teachers found it easier to work collaboratively during the COVID-19 crisis.

"Teachers are working smarter, not harder. … They're going digital to collaborate, brainstorm, and innovate with peers."

Patrick Hausammann
Supervisor of Instructional Technology/ITRT (instructional technology resource teacher)
Clarke County Public Schools, Berryville VA

"My wife … is the PreK-12 math coordinator in the district. She said (the pandemic) is forcing teachers and those co-teaching to focus on a single subject instead of multiple subjects."

Monty Hitschler
Director of Information Services and Technologies
Town of Rockport and Rockport Public Schools, Rockport MA

Teachers Were Under Pressure and Took on Remote Learning

It was not an easy time for teachers. The way they had been trained for a physical classroom, how they planned and assessed instruction, and even the time available for teaching changed suddenly. Many teachers had children of their own at home who had to be cared for and taught – all while they taught students. Days became long and packed with multiple responsibilities. Still, again and again, the educators interviewed praised their teachers.

"Teachers' efforts to reach kids have been extraordinary. We had to give permission to teachers to stop at 3 or 4 p.m. Some parents are available only in the evening. We encouraged teachers to take their evening time back."

Dr. Mike Muir
Learning through Technology Director
MSAD 44, Bethel ME

Recommendations:

When schools are moving through a crisis, success becomes all about effective teaching. An emergency can throw everything at a school or district into chaos, or it can provide an opportunity for growth. Professional development for teachers should be ongoing, and "just in time" for teachers going through remote emergency learning as well as online learning. During professional development or support sessions at schools, teachers should be encouraged to ask any question, even though it might seem basic.

Administrators should consider their teachers on the front line and provide them whatever they need for success, whether that is training, support, intervention with students or parents, or just a shoulder for crying. Successful schools polled teachers continually to assess their social-emotional health and provide support.

Schools need to address the digital homework gap between students. Funding is needed to alleviate this gap so that all children benefit from engaging teaching and learning with technology. The alternative of completing paper packets of handouts can be a dull experience. Several of the school leaders interviewed had to use this "low tech" method in a pinch. Some students will not complete and turn in the paper handouts, leading to a considerable learning gap.

If the school is to use technology for learning, all students must have access.

Technology and Technology Departments Got More Love and More Work (also see Chapter 8 - Cybersecurity)

It has been a long journey for education technologists. Some have labored for years, maybe decades, to share with teachers the vision of technology to enhance teaching and learning. Schools helped teachers to adapt and adjust by purchasing hardware and software and sponsoring professional development. Aside from core products, like the SIS, other products were often not mandated before the pandemic, so some teachers had continued to teach as they had been teaching for many years.

This scenario turned around fast once school buildings all over the world shut down. Teachers had to use technology to reach and see students directly. Schools mandated the use of video conferencing, LMS tools, and other products. Professional Development was delivered via video conferencing.

The technology department was the central facilitator of the shift to technology during this crisis. They got more love and respect from people than they ever had before. They also got a lot more work.

"It took the coronavirus for the technology department to get much-needed love from the Board of Directors and everyone else."

Larry Kahn
Chief Technology Officer
Trinity Valley School, Fort Worth TX

"My department has a design thinking specialist and education technologist giddy with the fact that every teacher is using technology—even the holdouts—and they are doing well. That's the biggest success story for us. Technology is on the main stage. How long have we been trying to get this?"- Darryl Loy

Summary:
- Technology in teaching and the technology departments in schools were in the spotlight, sometimes for the first time.
- Technology directors seized this moment to be sure teachers were supported and had the right professional development, that their staff was cared for and supported, and that they had a seat at the table running the school.

Recommendation:
- Seizing this moment of technology in the spotlight will help schools move online learning from a one-time endeavor into a new way to reach students. Carpe diem!

Food, Essentials, and Equity

Two student needs previously met with varying degrees of success in U.S. public schools became glaring: food insecurity and the homework gap/digital equity gap.

There has long been a well-known hunger and equity crisis in the U.S. Many children don't have enough to eat and qualify for one or two meals a day at school. Many students have neither digital devices for schoolwork, nor Internet access at home, yet teachers have been assigning homework that requires the

Internet. Until recently, students lacking Internet connectivity at home had gone to libraries, coffee shops, restaurants, and other locations to get work done. During the COVID-19 crisis, these alternate locations closed. Equity became an unmistakable need.

Meals for Students – Whether in U.S. District Schools or Not

Life in school is hard for many students. They struggle with the structure of school, academic expectations, the content of classes, and learning issues. Some students also have economic concerns, issues that impact nearly every aspect of a child's life. But at least many students who qualified could eat lunch and maybe breakfast at school five days a week. Students qualified for free or reduced lunch through the National School Lunch Program: reduced pricing when their annual family income was less than $40,764 for a family of four, and free meals when it was below $33,480 . In 2016, 30.4 million students qualified for free or reduced-price lunches in the U.S. See https://fns-prod.azureedge.net/sites/default/files/resource-files/NSLPFactSheet.pdf[1]

When schools closed for the pandemic emergency, suddenly there was no school-provided food for hungry children. Schools had to find a way to get that food to children in need.

Public school educators interviewed for this book described getting food to their kids as their #1 concern. They worried about the children who relied on getting breakfast and lunch outside the home. Schools came up with emergency plans, including having bus routes to deliver meals around their district. Staff at districts did not always differentiate whether children were attending school in the district or at local private or parochial schools; they just delivered food. Administrators sometimes did not ask whether students qualified. Many parents had lost their jobs, so providing food to children made sense.

---

1 USDA. *The National School Lunch Program Fact Sheet.* November 2017. accessed 7/30/20.

Some districts had drop-in times for any children or families to pick up food. Families were encouraged to go to whichever school was closest. Teachers sometimes staffed the drop-in food tables, and this gave them a chance to interact with students and families.

"We offered meals for all students 18 years or younger, whether they went to our school district or not. We provided mobile breakfast and lunch, with 7 or 8 bus routes with drivers delivering breakfast and lunch. The bus drivers would stay at each route until the designated announced time." – Victoria Andrews

"Our highest priority was making sure kids were fed. We're a high needs district. Kids rely on getting food." – MaryEllen Bunton

Infrastructure and Information in Place

The schools that had student devices, cloud computing to save files, schoolwide software, and accurate contact information for families had a smoother experience during the crisis of closed school buildings. Prior investments paid off during a stressful time.

Hardware, Training, and Software in Place

"The equipment, training, software we've purchased previously has paid off." – Monty Hitschler

"Having hardware resources in the hands of faculty and staff made transitioning that much easier." – James Huffaker

Schools that had not invested in 1-to-1 initiatives, cloud storage, and school licenses for software scrambled: they removed laptops from carts, spent budgets earmarked for other resources, and tried to provide devices and Internet access for every student. They knew that for online education to work, it had to work for every student. Schools found that reliable technology and data infrastructure were required to support their students who were learning at home.

Data on Families Needed to be Current – But Wasn't

School staff went to their records and started calling and emailing parents using the information they had on file. Staff, interns, paraprofessionals, and others were called into service to try to reach every family. It came to light that in many cases, information obtained when school had begun or when a child was first registered was no longer valid. School staff became creative at researching and finding data on parents. Without parent contact information, there was no checking up on students and families to see how they were coping, nor was there any way to track down students who didn't respond to teachers.

"Make sure all your data is right; it's hard to get ahold of people if you don't have the right phone numbers or emails." – Monty Hitschler

Recommendations:
- Technology audits should include software, hardware, and family data so that schools will be set up more solidly for future crises.
- Data and emergency contact lists need to be assessed frequently, not just once a year.

Digital Equity: The Homework Gap and Technology Tools

As many as 7 in 10 teachers assign homework requiring the Internet, yet many students don't have access at home. See this link for more information: https://www.aspeninstitute.org/blog-posts/the-homework-gap/.[2]

---

[2] Rosenworcel, Jessica. The Aspen Institute. *Millions of children can't do their homework because they don't have access to broadband internet.* June 30, 2016. accessed August 15, 2020.

Not all students had access to technology. The homework gap meant students without computing devices or Internet access at home or elsewhere couldn't participate in remote teaching. The digital equity gap increased during the coronavirus, as reported by EdSurge and other news sources. See https://www.edsurge.com/news/2020-06-16-covid-19-has-widened-the-homework-gap-into-a-full-fledged-learning-gap[3]. Technology-infused homework assignments left students behind.

Previously, students without Internet or devices accessed both by staying late at schools, visiting public libraries, or going online at Starbucks or McDonald's. Suddenly everything was closed. No school buildings, libraries, Starbucks, or McDonald's were open. The divide increased between students who had technology and those who did not, because of the closing of schools.

Like other schools, Payson quickly pointed network access points towards areas students could visit, including parking lots.

"We're opening schools in multiple areas with parking lots," – Victoria Andrews

"There's nothing like a national health crisis to put a glaring spotlight on digital inequality." – Dr. Mike Muir

"We're seeing inequities that government and business can't ignore." – Arline Pique

Schools experimented with creative solutions, including driving wireless access devices into neighborhoods. Students gathered around to do their homework and use the Wi-Fi signal.

Equipping buses with Wi-Fi temporarily provided Internet access. But how many of us would like to wait for the bus to arrive, then go outside in heat or

---

3 Tate, Emily. *COVID-19 Has Widened the 'Homework Gap' Into a Full-Fledged Learning Gap.* June 16, 2020. accessed August 1, 2020.

inclement weather to try to get homework done? This creative solution was a stopgap, but not a permanent solution.

A critical response during the pandemic in the U.S. was the CARES act passed by Congress to respond to economic issues caused by the COVID-19 crisis. Federal money was allocated as an economic stimulus to help people, businesses, schools, and organizations impacted by the pandemic. Schools benefitted from the CARES program. https://home.treasury.gov/policy-issues/cares[4]

Schools used CARES and other funds to purchase devices. Schools worked with local Internet providers to get access to students. Several large school districts went 1-to-1 for the first time. New York City, which had previously explored 1-to-1 learning but had not moved a 1-to-1 model for students, became the largest 1-to-1 district in the U.S. nearly overnight. https://gothamist.com/news/nyc-plans-feed-all-students-deliver-laptops-remote-learning[5] Philadelphia did the same and purchased laptops for students who had none. https://whyy.org/articles/equity-concerns-aside-philly-to-buy-laptops-for-all-students-for-virtual-classes/[6]

Recommendations:

Schools should expect and plan for the emergency preparation and distribution of food. The overhead of checking the qualifications of children will add an extra layer of complexity, so schools may want to skip this step. Food distribution plans should ensure that supply chains can accommodate emergency demand.

Schools should check which students have a digital device and which students need one. This crisis bumped 1-to-1 (1 child assigned to 1 computer) from an

---

4 U.S. Department of the Treasury. *The CARES Act Works for All Americans.* n.d. accessed August 2, 2020.

5 Chang, Sophia. Gothamist. *NYC Plans to Feed All Students, Deliver Laptops for Remote Learning.* March 16, 2020. accessed July 31, 2020.

6 Wolfman-Arent, Avi, WHYY PBS. *Philly to buy laptops for needy students for virtual classes during shutdown.* March 24, 2020. accessed July 15, 2020.

option to a necessity. The workarounds, like bus-enabled Wi-Fi, might work for a short while. The longer-term solution is thinking of digital devices and the Internet as being as necessary as textbooks.

Parents Gained New Respect for Teachers

From social media memes to parent group discussions, teachers were getting new respect from parents who suddenly had to manage their work and home lives while helping their children complete schoolwork. People began to see the difficult job teachers have, and what an art it is to reach students and help them learn.

"What might be different is that the teaching profession is revered again, and people see the importance of it. Not everyone can be a teacher. We need to love on them. It's a critical job." – MaryEllen Bunton

Recommendations:

Schools or districts should understand that what teachers do is not always appreciated by parents until those parents have to manage their child's learning at home.

Schools need to tell their own "good news" stories by reporting on the positive efforts of teachers, highlighting examples of their courage and professionalism. Some schools use Twitter hash tags and share posts of this nature on Facebook, Instagram and their own Web pages.

An anti-teacher backlash has surfaced in some areas of the U.S. as of the writing of this book. School administrators are weighing whether they will return fully face-to-face, with a hybrid or blended learning approach, or entirely online. Movie theatres, houses of worship, and restaurants have only partially opened in some U.S. states, yet some schools might reopen. COVID-19 is a deadly virus that has killed thousands of people in the U.S. and sickened millions more. People are disparaging reluctant teachers on social media. Educators are considering impossible choices – go to work and risk their safety, or lose their jobs and income. Schools are reopening and then closing again. This uncertainty is not helpful and should be addressed.

Here's an article from northjersey.com written in early September, 2020 describing the backlash against teachers: https://www.northjersey.com/story/news/education/2020/09/03/nj-schools-coronavirus-teachers-feel-backlash-over-remote-learning-push/5684988002/[7]

It's my opinion that it's not the parents who praised teachers now critiquing worried teachers. I would encourage those with sympathetic voices to give teachers grace for their worry. Let the voices of those who see the good that teachers have done, be the loudest.

Parents, Including Teachers Who Are Parents, Had a Tough Time

Everyone living through the pandemic crisis awoke to a new world. Parents found their children were home all day every day instead of at school. They had to figure out how to support this new dynamic. Parents might have been working from home, or perhaps were suddenly unemployed, or perhaps they were essential workers. The latter had to be on the front line at hospitals, grocery stores, and other institutions and did not have the option of staying home, no matter how young their children were. Juggling responsibilities for children became the new norm. Teachers who were parents had to support their children at home, plus they had to plan and deliver lessons to the students they taught.

"Parents were more active, whether they wanted to be or not." – *Suzy Brooks*

---

[7] Adely, Hannan, Northernjersey.com, *Once hailed as heroes, NJ teachers face backlash as tensions grow over all-remote learning*, September 3, 2020, accessed September 7, 2020.

"The biggest thing is to really offer an abundance of grace and flexibility to faculty, students, and parents because it is an unprecedented time in our lives. There's no way to know what every student and family is going through. We have to extend that grace. It's okay. Kids could have a sick parent at home. A lot of our families have both parents who are doctors. We extend grace to those families."- Darryl Loy

Recommendations:

Ways to alleviate the tremendous stress experienced by teachers and parents during a crisis should be part of the crisis plan by a school. Schools should extend grace, concern, support, and understanding to employees, students, and parents alike.

For Remote Teaching and Learning, the Schedule Must Change

The difference between teaching and learning in a physical school versus remotely became abundantly clear when schools moved to online learning. Scheduling drove so much in physical schools, including time, classes, activities, availability of teachers and co-teachers, rooms and shared spaces, breakfast, lunch, dismissals, and bus arrivals and departures. These elements disappeared when schools moved to remote learning as learning happened at home and not in school buildings.

Schedules needed to change and adapt for online teaching and learning. Students and teachers were not able to spend a full school day of seven or more hours on remote learning, either synchronously or asynchronously. Administrators decided that having teachers or students in front of a screen for multiple video sessions was exhausting for all participants. It was also detrimental both emotionally and physically. There was even a new phrase, "Zoom fatigue", that was coined during the pandemic.

"This is a great chance to change schedules. It's been an introduction to what distance learning can look like and how we can give more opportunities to the different way schedules change day-to-day."

Tye Campbell
Director of Technology
Gilman School, Baltimore MD

"You can't expect teachers to mimic the same school day. It's not realistic. Those challenges are around getting teachers to flip their mindset and the level of expectations."

Milena Streen
VP and Chief Information Officer
St Ignatius High School, Cleveland OH

Recommendations:

Replicating a 7-hour daily schedule when learning became remote doesn't work. Students can't be in front of screens that long. It has been found that instruction instead works best if varied between synchronous and asynchronous, between whole class, small group, and 1-on-1 instruction. Flexibility is important. Assessing what concepts needed further teaching and having classes just for those students who needed to reinforce the knowledge in question worked well. This technique should be remembered.

Students Learned Resilience

Resilience has long been an attribute we have wanted students to learn. It equips young people to deal with the ups and downs of life, and makes them better prepared emotionally for the next roller coaster ride. To this end, teachers often provided case studies, lessons, and examples, hoping that students would gain an understanding of the importance of resilience.

Students all around the world living through the COVID-19 crisis suddenly had to deal with uncertainty, lack of structure, the elimination of events and activities, and economic concerns as their parents might have lost their jobs. It was the worst kind of roller coaster, and it happened in a matter of days.

"For this group of kids, especially seniors, my kids in college, they will be resilient moving forward. We've been teaching students how to be resilient here at Ravenscroft as part of our Lead From Here citizen leader program, but these kids will be incredibly resilient and able to handle tough situations rather than kids that didn't go through this. Examples of handling disappointment - incredible disappointment. The level of disappointment and handling in the future will make them stronger, and they will see life differently."

> *Jason Ramsden*
> *Chief Information Officer*
> *Ravenscroft School, Raleigh NC*

When Mr. Apel was asked about what students were experiencing and thinking about their future, he cited *What's the Dealio*, a podcast the students have created. One episode focused on what students were thinking about as they lived through an extraordinary time. They had to leave school quickly and not return during the school year; some would not be coming back at all. This student podcast episode is especially relevant – the word "resilient" is used by the students to describe their own experiences when everything in school suddenly shifted:

https://podcasts.apple.com/us/podcast/whats-the-dealio/id1478489078[8]

> *Warren Apel*
> *Director of Technology*
> *The American School in Japan, Tokyo*

Recommendations:

Parents and teachers should carefully and kindly support students who have gone through a significant crisis. The activities and events they perceived as

---

[8] Apple Podcasts. What's the Dealio?. *2019-20: Year in Review.* June 9, 2020. accessed July 7, 2020.

routine changed overnight. Having a perspective on the situation and developing resilience is essential and will help children's future emotional health.

> ▶ **School Leadership Committee Takeaway**
> The stories and learnings from the educators interviewed likely resonated with your leadership committee. You may have thought of stories from your teachers, administrators, parents, and students.
> - As you debrief from the end of 2020 and plan the next school year, are there venues for hearing stories from your stakeholders?
>   - Can teachers share their experiences, can students write about and present their remote emergency learning stories?
>   - Will there be time during future faculty meetings, parent meetings, whole school, or district meetings to share?
>   - Can you create a Coronavirus Chronicle of your own to relate experiences and to save for the future?
> - The learnings for this chapter are in hierarchical order according to what educators felt was most important.
>   - What was your hierarchy of needs for your school community?
>   - Would that hierarchy be the same or different in other crises or during a regular school year?

Chapter 3 – Social-Emotional Health & Learning

Introduction

There was no question about social-emotional health posed in the educators' interview, yet the topic was brought up repeatedly as a concern. Educators were worried about students, teachers, parents, administrators, and staff while everyone's world upended quickly. They wondered how people would cope now that regular social interactions had stopped, and there was so much uncertainty.

Ethan Delavan is a technology director who has earned the respect of his colleagues through his knowledge about and interest in social-emotional health. Ethan kindly agreed to write this chapter.

Social-Emotional Health and a School Crisis

> Ethan Delavan
> Director of Technology
> The Bush School, Seattle WA

A World Turned Upside Down

We've heard families, students, and colleagues say that the COVID-19 pandemic turned their world upside down. This expresses the grief that comes with a sudden loss of normalcy. Those of us with stronger social-emotional skills can navigate this grief with more calmness and tenacity, persevering through change and bouncing back more readily to a new normal.

What are those skills that offer us greater resilience? How do social-emotional learning (SEL) practitioners inculcate these skills in students? What can educational leaders do proactively to support the SEL efforts of the schools in which we work?

I spoke with three SEL practitioners in different school settings in America to home in on some answers to these questions. Kimberlee Williams was a co-director of diversity, equity, and inclusion, as well as a Spanish teacher, at a day and boarding high school on the East Coast during the pandemic. Gayle Gingold is a counselor at an independent K-12 school (as well as a marriage and family therapist) on the West Coast. Laura Potter was a school psychologist in a large urban public district in the Midwest and is currently transitioning to educational research at the university level.

What Do We Mean by *Social-Emotional*?

Beyond our lay understanding of mental health or a happy social life, social-emotional health encompasses several important facets. Schools are increasingly seeing the need to directly address the learning that supports students' social-emotional wellbeing if anything like traditional academic success is to be expected of them. Approaches to SEL vary, but all of them share a core path from self-awareness to self-regulation in a collaborative social context. The focus on context conceptualizes an individual student not as a separable unit, but rather a growing part of an ever-expanding flow of interpersonal exchange and influence.

Williams emphasizes the intercultural facet of SEL. She defines it as the ability to engage across difference in a way that is healthy, productive, empathic, and successful. When a student is comfortable reaching out to and hearing from those who are different from them, this speaks to a stamina for self-regulation that students have developed over time. It takes a great deal of self-awareness to manage one's own emotional triggers in group interactions, especially those that span significant cultural differences; and an awareness of cultural norms enables students to engage with people unlike themselves in a variety of ways.

Gingold emphasizes the empathic component of SEL. This begins with cultivating in students an awareness of others' emotions, with the eventual aim of having them take the perspective of others. The capacity for flexible thinking engendered by this practice is another facet of social-emotional health. Adults that are too binary or rigid in their thinking can experience problems connecting with others, especially with those very different from them.

Ideally, social-emotional curricula do not operate solely outside traditional school curricula or only as an add-on class. Successful SEL programs give students a conscious focus on the landscape of their own social-emotional life, while emphasizing its relevance in all subject areas. Williams notes the occasional need for a teacher to pause a content-oriented lesson plan in order to take care of an emerging social-emotional need felt among members of the class in the moment. Teachers may, on very short notice, find themselves in charge of creating a safe space in which students can productively express anger or cry, becoming gradually more comfortable with unfamiliar emotions expressed productively in a social context. Because of this, buy-in among faculty is critical to the success of an SEL initiative, and best practices around implementing SEL encourage even the highest level of school leadership to commit to the relevance of emotional intelligence to their own professional lives.

SEL should begin in elementary grades and be strongly supported by teachers of young children. But, in Williams' words, "the need for that instruction doesn't go away after lower school. Some of my best college professors were those that brought up these tough topics for you to grapple with, but at the same time held your hand in a way that said, 'I'm going to teach you how to manage your emotions and your thoughts that are triggered by you reading this really intense stuff.'"

Potter, in a large district, has turned her attention to how leadership can consistently implement SEL throughout its diverse settings. The work necessary to establish this shared awareness in students should begin long before a school faces a crisis disruptive of interactional normalcy, as early and consistent social-emotional support of students is the backstop that allows teachers to remain related to, and supportive of, students who find themselves adrift in a new situation. Several frameworks for implementing SEL in schools exist, and some will be more germane to the school's pedagogy than others.

Let's take a quick glance at how some of these frameworks differ.

Breaking Down SEL

Success in relating SEL to academic work and lifelong learning is more likely when all faculty are on board with the initiative, including training in the SEL framework of choice, experience interacting with peers in the context of the framework, and practice in guiding students to use the framework. The three discussed here are not intended to be an exhaustive list but rather to highlight some of the illustrative differences.

First, the Institute for Social and Emotional Learning emerged from work at the Nueva School in California. The approach here is decidedly experiential, focusing on activities that may appear traditionally academic on the surface, but also challenging students to examine their emotional responses as the activity unfolds. This framework encourages teachers to engage students in highly interactive problem-solving or dramatic games, with a healthy dose of journal-based introspection.

This approach intersects with Carol Dweck's work on growth mindset, which explicitly asks students to see intelligence not as a fixed ability, but rather as a skill achieved by practice whose application is under the student's control when they undertake the effort. A growth mindset releases a student from the need to prove their innate capacity, allowing them to better relate to others around them.

Second, the RULER system was developed at the Yale Center for Emotional Intelligence, led by Marc Brackett. A more analytical system, it encourages students to name and understand their emotions. A common tagline is "Name it to tame it," which encourages students to label their emotions and think consciously about how to regulate their participation in school activities. The RULER acronym stands for actions that a student takes toward their own emotions:

- Recognizing
- Understanding
- Labeling
- Expressing
- Regulating

Among the tools of the RULER system is the Mood Meter, which is both a quadrant graph and a phone app. The graph compares pleasantness along one axis with energy along the other, and the app suggests names (labels) for each of the dot points (moods) that a person might be feeling at the time. Some teachers have a copy of the chart in their rooms, and young children may check in by placing a token that reflects their mood. Teachers of older students may reference the chart and check in verbally with members of the class to get a sense of how to adjust their lesson that day.

Third, the Collaborative for Academic, Social, and Emotional Learning (CASEL) frames SEL efforts in a whole-community context. CASEL identifies five domains of competency in social-emotional health:

- Self-awareness
- Self-management
- Social awareness
- Relationship skills
- Responsible decision-making

These domains are wrapped in three tiers of student support: The classroom provides SEL curriculum and instruction. The school or district provides effective practices and policies. And the home and larger community present opportunities for partnership, which become all the more important when the normalcy of the school day is disrupted.

Whatever the framework, systematizing SEL in a way germane to school and district needs allows a school to prioritize SEL curricula, teachers to adopt consistent lesson plans quickly, and students to develop their own understanding of themselves as emerging actors in the world. During a disruption, such frameworks enable schools to elect either to shift priority to another aspect of social-emotional wellbeing, or to reorganize resources around the priorities they had set beforehand.

Implementing SEL

Using CASEL well before the crisis, Potter worked with a team of her colleagues to create slide decks for teachers to use during advisory sessions lead by teachers. This relieved teachers of the burden of creating their own social-emotional prompts and enabled shared inquiry and vocabulary among the entire student body. She and her team could focus on one or two competencies at a time, allowing for cross-pollination of experience among teachers, as well as a deeper understanding among students of what that component meant.

Using RULER at her independent school, Gingold and her peers in the Support Services department work both with teachers assigned to deliver a multi-faceted Human Relations (HR) curriculum to students during designated class times, as well as with classroom teachers. Among the issues explored in HR are digital identity and social media. Much of the discussion during advisory times, led by teachers in smaller groups, centers around the social-emotional experience of the students, helping them to find ways to share and normalize each other's feelings.

As communication and socialization in our culture become inexorably more digitally mediated, it is the province of technology leaders in schools to understand the SEL goals of the institution and take a hand in guiding systems, deployments, and professional development in a way that aligns with the relationship-centric aims of SEL. This baseline not only normalizes the framework as a method for building the interactive stamina that Williams describes but also allows teachers to adapt the framework to a disrupted—and necessarily technologized—environment with a deeper understanding of how it will impact students' social-emotional health.

Hitting the Skids

"Disruption to normalcy," says Williams, "leads to every negative emotion or state of being we can name. We are creatures of connection, and feeling as isolated as we do [during the COVID-19 quarantine] is just not normal. We're not prepared for this. Going in with that assumption might inform how we interact with one another and with the students online."

Young people are in various stages of figuring out where (or even whether) they belong. When a school's traditional ways of centering student experience break down, students need something to reassure them that they still matter. Schools unprepared to make this pivot quickly can leave their staff with the frustration of feeling overwhelmed and powerless. This powerlessness is acutely felt by those directly responsible for the social-emotional learning and wellbeing of students, since monitoring social-emotional issues is often achieved by observing in-person behaviors. The powerlessness felt by SEL practitioners speaks to a sudden breakdown of the school's ability to assess and respond to the social-emotional needs of students, even at a time when the students may need it most.

Social-emotional skills are about navigating a community context. When a crisis occurs, the context that community members are navigating changes radically. In preparing for a long-term disruption of the in-school experience, both administrators and educational technologists need to consider the nature and importance of social-emotional learning in academic success. Attending to systems and processes that maintain the school's ability to measure social-emotional wellbeing can buoy SEL practitioners' capacity to have an impact at a distance.

Family as the Learning Environment

As soon as a school campus closes, the focus becomes the social-emotional health of the family in which the student lives. By way of comparison, pediatricians often speak of the mother-infant dyad, a relationship upon which the eventual independent health of the child depends. In the early hours after birth and during infancy, many pediatricians attend to the health of the bond between mother and child, rather than simply the health indicators of either one.

Schools in a campus closure are in a similar position of helping to foster the efficacy of the home learning environment, upon which the students' maturation and learning now more heavily depend. Potter notes that training students in the use of online tools that suddenly became central to the flow of their learning was a major hurdle for schools that had not already undertaken technology literacy programs and perhaps moved to a 1:1 model of computing. Learning technical skills haphazardly—and while content-area assignments are also due—can have an impact on a student's perception of their own abilities. Schools may wish to consider a means of assessing how ready their students are to navigate online tools that support their education. Indeed, online tools may become the backbone of the new normal that precedes the next crisis. Integral to this backbone is a clear set of expectations for online conduct and engagement that a school must set for students.

Parents themselves need support in a situation such as a school closure. Schools and districts may wish to consider how they will support the needs of parents as integral to the social-emotional and academic success of students. Potter saw some frustration among teachers who did not hear back from parents about some of their students, and there was no specific recourse in place to address this important part of the bond that supports social-emotional development. Much of this support simply has to do with how to navigate technology, understand a child's progress, and reach out to the school with questions. Finally, Gingold notes that the family as a social-emotional unit may need support from the school to undergo the reorganization that is necessary to address the changes in normalcy and reset expectations about what counts as enough. Centralizing this function in a way that is appropriate to the size of the district or school will support the total social-emotional wellbeing of the family unit.

Reaching Out – School Teams

Effective mental health teams may comprise psychologists, counselors, social workers, human relations teachers, and nurses. During school closures, it can be effective for these teams to leverage the same learning management systems in use by teachers. This allows them a great deal of control over the content on these sites, to ensure alignment with the SEL framework of choice and with the emerging needs of their student body. As students are already familiar with the learning platform, teaching them to navigate it is not a hurdle, and it feels more like one of their classes, engendering the sense that this is important information in itself.

However, the ease of control for SEL practitioners should not supersede the best practice of weaving SEL explorations into the overall curriculum. For example, if the mental health team can integrate their efforts with that of classroom teachers, SEL "warm-ups" or other brief inquiries can be integrated with necessary touchpoints such as daily attendance, advisory, or tutoring times. In this regard, a learning environment managed solely by SEL practitioners can come to be a resource for teachers looking to integrate SEL activities, as well as for students.

Checking Normalcy

Methods of enabling students to self-refer for social-emotional support can become even more important and challenging during a school closure. Potter and her team began by posting their contact information in their online classroom and received almost no responses. This may have had to do with the level of discomfort that young teenagers naturally feel about picking up the phone or beginning an email from scratch. And they may not yet have developed the verbal skills that help them advocate without prompting for their own social-emotional wellbeing. Email, in general, often proved to be an ineffective way to reach out for several reasons. Today's youth have moved beyond email to more immediate and social forms of exchange, making email appear old and cumbersome to them. And many schools still do not have cogent digital literacy curricula to ensure that students understand processes and expectations in different communication media.

Building on success touted by teachers using online fillable forms to solicit feedback from students, Potter and her team changed course, creating an online form where students had only to click on the issues that applied to them, including an option "just to talk." Dozens of students used the form and self-identified as needing support. Having enough information to begin a discussion, members of Potter's team could then follow up with students ready for adult intervention. Said Potter, "It's funny how different it was just to have a form that they could just click, versus having to actually take the initiative to write an email or call a teacher. I think they felt really uncomfortable with that." The online form may also have the effect of normalizing the students' feelings from the outset, since clickable choices tend to reify emotional issues as common and understandable.

Initially unable to get a reading of her students' emotional wellbeing at a distance, Gingold also made use of an online form she called a Wellness Check, which all students would fill out weekly on the same day, during small-group advisory. They did not need to tell their advisors what they were writing into the form, only give the thumbs-up on video chat after they submitted it. Generally, the form contained the same questions each week, unless Gingold saw a trend about which she wanted deeper information. Students could request to be contacted, and Gingold sometimes reached out on her own initiative if something in a student's responses warranted follow-up.

Williams notes that we are used to asking each other cursorily *How are you?* This is often little more than a greeting, especially in American culture, and there is usually only the scripted response of *fine* or *good*. In an in-person situation, a teacher might pick up on body language or other attentional cues as red flags for checking in with the emotional health of a student, but in a remote or disrupted setting this is harder to do, possibly leaving teachers with a false impression of a student's emotional state. Instead, Williams recommends asking, specifically, how students are managing this lack of normalcy and how their teachers might best show up for them in this crisis.

If students have not yet developed the self-awareness to be able to articulate what they're feeling, they may be very willing to tell you what they're thinking about. "Great," says Gingold, "let's start there, because with thoughts and emotions, there's more and more research saying it doesn't really matter so much what came first. They really inform each other."

Delivering Care

Independent schools often have latitude to create ways of connecting with students that suit the existing infrastructure of the school and the needs of the SEL practitioners. When the school counselor is no longer just at the end of the hallway, it is important to offer adjusted tools to maintain both actual availability to students, as well as the implicit reassurance of someone there when a student needs them. Mirroring the ease of use that Potter's form offered, Gingold and her team pivoted quickly to a calendar integration service that advertised open slots in a counselor's digital calendar and allowed students to reserve a time that suited them. These appointments then appeared in the student's calendar if they were versed in keeping their appointments online.

Potter's school had a different challenge as a public middle school in a large urban district. Her population included upwards of eighty percent of students on free and reduced lunch. The hurdles that families face in this socio-economic bracket can make it difficult for the school to contact students. Fewer devices in the household, for example, meant less time for the student to be available for distance communication, and these families were more often considered essential workers or held jobs that were not workable from home. If the family relied on only one or two mobile phones, rather than a landline as well, then there was no guarantee that reaching a parent led to reaching a student. "There were so many students who just fell off the map," lamented Potter, "and they were students who had previously tuned in really well at school." This situation, all too common for many large districts, leaves staff without a cohesive understanding of the social-emotional wellbeing of their students, even as that wellbeing may be under particular stress.

Some schools choose to or are required to use various filtering technologies to limit access to inappropriate content and monitor student activity, including emails and other text that they generate under the school's systems. Though she found some of its use problematic from a privacy standpoint, Potter did appreciate the ability of her school's monitoring software to send reports of certain keywords, such as *suicide*. This allowed her team to identify some students who were experiencing suicidal ideation and make interventions. Deliberation and transparency are important in deciding whether and how to deploy these tools, as they are not a substitute for trusting relationships between students and adults.

Diversity and Social-Emotional Expectations

"So much of my work is bringing people together to talk," muses Williams, who felt as if compounding crises had turned her professional world upside down. Online communication methods left people feeling more self-conscious and reluctant to engage, even as increasing racial tensions emphasized the urgency of Williams' job function. She set out to create an online space and culture that could offer similar opportunities for engagement, as did on-campus venues. Similar to Potter's experience, this was not just a "build it, and they will come" proposition.

Since a crisis situation necessarily puts teachers and support staff more closely in touch with parents and guardians of diverse backgrounds, it becomes important for faculty and staff to be aware of their social location, an exercise of their own emotional intelligence. As most K-12 teachers are white, it becomes important to identify what privileges and disadvantages that affords them in different situations. As white teachers work more specifically to understand their own white cultural lens, they can begin to better understand the needs and perspectives of families of color. For example, following the lead of the parents in these situations can defuse the assumption that a school's social-emotional practitioner is coming in as the expert, thereby missing cultural norms and cues that are important to the social-emotional health of the family. SEL practitioners might begin by inquiring of the family what support they need and tuning their efforts to the family's responses.

In independent schools, where students of color may still form a minority of the student body, a teacher's time, and attention in reaching out personally, may be critical to the feeling of belonging experienced by a student of color. What teachers do or fail to do sends specific messages, especially to students of color. Says Williams, "If you have not reached out individually to a kid of color to say *I know that this is on your mind. What do you need from me?* then you are saying to that kid: *I don't care.*" Williams developed a script that freed faculty from having to guess at what overtures might work best between white faculty and students of color, as well as helping to ensure a baseline of engagement for all of these students. Schools should consider working with diversity, equity, and inclusion leaders to develop such scripts and protocols that can be quickly activated and adapted to closure situations or other national crises.

The one-to-one connections can end up supporting the efficacy of the larger online spaces that Williams set out to create, such as all-school or grade-level meetings over video conference. Williams received repeated feedback that her teachers' overtures were met with real appreciation from students. Once a student is aware, through personal interactions, that their voice matters to adults at the school, they can be more comfortable, open, and honest in large group discussions. The initial step of personal interaction allows them to find more meaning in these large online events, which can seem overwhelming and disorganized at first.

Identified Academic Issues

Remote schooling can be especially difficult for students with executive function issues, such as ADD/ADHD or anxiety. For these students, making a transition from one activity to another without the usual in-school cues can be difficult. When such a student has their own personal computer, staying focused can come to feel almost impossible for them, and managing transitions from one task to another can be frustrating. For these students, articulating a structure to follow and bringing parents in to help manage this rhythm was key. The ability of SEL to offer students more sophisticated vocabulary for what they're feeling can, over time, allow students to self-regulate in ways that affirm their emotional skills, rather than pin them to a diagnosis.

Students with identified learning disabilities often struggled in a remote context, as they did not have access to the usual tools and supports afforded at their schools. Gingold encouraged parents to focus on validating what a student did well on a given day. That is, rather than focusing on productivity as a goal, having a student identify what they did well, no matter how trivial, can build self-regulation. "Productivity, when there's a lack of motivation," says Gingold, "leads right into people not feeling good enough—and shame."

Families of English language learners are a major facet of many school districts, and teachers often noted the special difficulty of ensuring that this family was ready to support a home learning environment. Translators may be available to parents who don't speak English, but they are often overwhelmed by the need for so much one-to-one support. This often leaves the student in a partially parentalized role, as they need not only to translate for their parents but also to explain the cultural significance of what the school is asking of the family. In all situations, and especially these, it is important for schools to engage parents in understanding the goals for SEL and how parents can reinforce these lessons and draw on these tools as a family. At the same time, social-emotional practitioners themselves should strive to step outside their own cultural assumptions to meet families where they are.

Gingold emphasizes that a major component of social-emotional health is knowing when you need help and whom to go to for this. In order to destigmatize the act of seeking help, schools may need to focus extra care on families whose students have executive function issues or who may not yet know how to navigate the prevailing culture in their school district. This outreach can begin to instill confidence in families that help is available and that they can model for their children how to initiate social interactions that lead to the resolution of strong emotions.

Family Stressors

Being stuck at home with family for most or all of the day can be a mixed blessing for students. "Your home can be a place of refuge and comfort and joy and laughter and peace… Or it can be just a place you lay your head." In the latter case, says Williams, "you haven't had the practice of engaging with your family members, because most of your waking hours you spend with other people, traditionally." Quarantine at home can itself open a new chapter in social-emotional learning. Interacting with parents can be emotionally fraught, as they may need to be working or may not have the tutoring skills necessary to guide a child's learning. Gingold observed some gendered trends in this regard, where the inevitable extra tasks that come with homebound schooling often fell to the mother in a heterosexual household, thereby causing increased marital tension. And a student's resentment of the disrupture of normalcy can often be laid on their parents, as children may implicitly or openly blame them for being unable to go to school.

Without a designated way to reach groups of students, Potter and her team pivoted quickly, finding videos that could be easily shared with students to surface ideas for how to deal with emotions that came with being surrounded by family for much more of the day than normal. This delivery of basic skills afforded students the vocabulary that they could begin using as they checked in with teachers through online means and regulated their participation in distance learning environments.

Other emotions Gingold discovered were frustration in navigating technological tools or getting enough access to technology. Students also felt overwhelmed by what they perceived to be a heavier workload than during normal schooling. Some felt unproductive or unmotivated, and others worried that the crisis would affect them directly, with them or a family member falling ill from COVID-19.

Though many students reported feeling tired, bored or drained by remote school, students surveyed by schools also reported feeling less overall stress once the rhythm of remote schooling settled in, and they characterized themselves as more content. Since these surveys were largely informal, it would be interesting to delve deeper into this dichotomy. Were these two disparate groups of students or the same students at different moments? Or did students perhaps find themselves feeling both states at the same time? What circumstances might allow more students to experience the contentment of a more relaxed routine, which stood out as one of the few benefits of being in quarantine?

Coping and Resilience

Both Gingold and Williams noticed several families who had already developed positive coping skills, and these families fared relatively well without the normal routine of school. Still, says Gingold, "I do worry about the impact of the isolation that COVID-19 is bringing. What is that going to do to their development? It's so important for them to be around their peers for so many reasons. It's just as important as academics."

Indeed, students universally reported missing their friends. Friendships are key for students, especially as they enter the years of middle and high school. As young teenagers often feel like outsiders, the feedback students receive from friends helps to normalize their own struggles and to remind them that they are not alone. For students who are exploring identities such as LGBTQ, their friend group can offer support and normalcy for their identity formation that their family might not. "Not having regular social contact with peers in real life," says Gingold, "relying on electronic communication with an undeveloped prefrontal cortex, it amplified a lot of feelings of being an outsider or not being good enough."

Though she saw some students settle into the disrupted rhythm, Williams said she saw more go from bad to worse. This is another reason that personal connections are so important to establish before a crisis situation. Whether it's an advisor, coach, counselor, or homeroom teacher, a trusted adult outside the home is key to setting social-emotional learning in the home on a solid footing.

Gingold noticed marked increases in anxiety and depression. Suicidality, she notes, goes up significantly during any time of crisis, and disrupted schooling is no different. Teachers and advisors are the first line of defense in recognizing when a student may be moving toward thoughts of giving up. These are often expressed in comments spoken aloud by students, such as feeling depressed or wondering *What's the point?* Many of these red flags came from discussions around questions that Gingold fed to small-group advisors to ask their students. Advisors could report concerning statements to Gingold, who could then establish a bridge to that student, sometimes coaching the advisor in how to reach out further.

Gingold's school collaborates with a locally available program called Forefront Suicide Prevention Center. This group offers both onsite trainings in how to nurture sustaining relationships with students and discuss personal matters, as well as training in how to develop these kinds of relationships during distance learning. This program is a natural complement to SEL, as it emphasizes building the same frameworks for emotional regulation as do more general SEL frameworks. Schools may wish to establish connections with local suicide prevention agencies and ensure that teachers understand how to identify a concerning trend in a student's thinking and to refer that appropriately.

One of the most important lessons for students involved in an upset of their normalcy is that they have the power of resilience. These disruptions are an opportunity for them to flex their emotional muscles in ways that a predictable school setting may not especially engender. The combination of witnessing their teachers making the best of a bad situation, along with the need to marshal their own internal resources, has the potential to leave students with a sense of themselves as strong agents of stability in their own lives.

Williams has noticed that white students tend to have less developed resilience muscles and may respond to a crisis by denying their own emotional reactions to it. Requests for medication and the incidence of depression go up significantly during crises like the COVID-19 pandemic. She notes that trauma-informed care reminds us that students of different backgrounds respond to the same crisis very differently. Prior to a crisis, schools may wish to undertake a study of how they might expect their students to respond in an emergent situation that precipitates a loss of normalcy.

Working with students to develop their own practices of self-care in advance of a crisis can build the resilience muscle to carry them through difficult situations. Gingold notes that young teenagers, especially, are likely to believe they're the only one having these feelings. Tools as simple as coloring, choosing calming music, and journaling, exercise, or building online communities can help form habits of self-awareness and interpersonal engagement that reassure them that, as Williams says, "we are not passing through this storm alone."

Large school districts have a need to systematize more formally what an independent school might improvise. Potter was responsible for assessing students with special education needs and for collaborating with peers to create multi-tiered systems of support. These were intended to integrate academic and behavioral concerns. In this setting, school psychologists may be seen as administrators, helping to make decisions around equity and engagement or instructional leadership.

Tracking Relationships

Part of a school's resilience during an extended closure or disruption of normalcy rests on its ability to continue the learning experience and the context of care that students encounter on campus. To this end, databases that accurately represent effective ways to contact both guardians and students are a vital tool in creating an equitable educational environment. Schools may want to consider fields and data collection methods that allow SEL practitioners to quickly understand the family situation of a student when the need arises, rather than having to begin that research in a crisis situation. Even with *emergency contact* field sets, few student information systems include layouts that efficiently capture this information with an eye toward an extended closure; but most systems will allow for the creation of custom fields. Larger school districts and independent school associations should consider what array of fields would benefit this goal and pressure database providers to enhance a school's ability to understand how best to engage with each particular family. To this end, database providers might take a cue from fundraising database schema, which allow for detailed notes about each encounter with a donor, including preferred ways of approaching them.

For families living in poverty, the need for schools to stay abreast of their contact information is greater, as these families move residence and change phone numbers more often. Waiting for a crisis to update lines of communication with these families can put these children especially at risk of experiencing social-emotional issues. Since such families' primary device may be a cell phone, it's important that any online access for parents be easily viewed and manipulated on this size of screen. Finally, training parents and guardians in the use of the online portal is critical, as some of them may not initially see it as useful nor be sure how to navigate it.

As we look into the longer term of preparedness, Gingold recommends surveying students about what they're facing emotionally as a window into how schools might set reasonable goals and expectations. These results can focus a school's crisis preparedness efforts, both by offering a baseline for how students experience themselves emotionally during normal schooling and also by identifying what areas of weakness exist in the school's efforts to instill resilience through SEL.

Telepresence for SEL

The relatively recent maturation of easily accessible, high-quality video conferencing systems, Williams notes, was a tremendous relief in coping with the disruption of closure. Video solutions that allow for a wide range of controls and modes of feedback were generally preferred by teachers, especially those that allowed teachers to tighten or loosen their own levels of control based on the age and social-emotional integrity of their students.

Also popular were video conferencing tools that could display all or nearly all participants at once. As large-group meetings played a role in maintaining the group identity of some schools, the ability for students to page quickly through a few screens and see all of their peers lent a sense of togetherness that was otherwise at risk of fading from memory.

Further, the ability of some video conferencing platforms to allow for various forms of nonverbal feedback, whiteboarding, and user-controlled view modes means that a district's or school's choice of video platform is not a trivial matter.

For the purposes of social-emotional health meetings, not all video conference platforms are Health Insurance Portability and Accountability Act (HIPAA) compliant. In some cases, this has to do with the nature of the platform's security. In other cases, such as many free platforms, this lack of compliance can boil down to the lack of business agreement between the school and the vendor. There is some value in using the same platform as students use in their online work to avoid their having to navigate a different interface. However, one-on-one meetings with an advisor or counselor can be conducted with different and simpler in-browser video platforms that may lack advanced participant management features.

The activities possible in a remote situation with video conferencing and other rich-media platforms can offer new horizons for SEL. Students can bring others into their gardens or rooms, insofar as they are comfortable. Some students who may be reluctant to speak directly about their emotions may reveal a lot to social-emotional practitioners in how they share artifacts of their personal lives. As long as teachers are sensitive to the equity and status issues this can trigger, home-based sharing can have the effect of bringing together students who wouldn't ordinarily have come to know each other.

Different students will engage with different aspects of the media. Seeing other students visually can reify a feeling of shared experience. Or the opportunity for a student to type concerns into a chat stream might be less intimidating that speaking it out loud. Williams leverages different avenues afforded by technology in asking her students to contribute their "roses and thorns" in the chat while in the same video conference they may discuss these conflicting experiences orally.

Screen fatigue, however, is a problem. Gingold notes that this comes from the cognitive dissonance of having the appearance of being with others but knowing that no one is actually together. The need for heightened awareness of nonverbal cues and the extra cognition it takes to interpret them is exhausting for the mind and the body. Add to this that many students were expected to sit at their computers for hours a day, first in synchronous classes and then for asynchronous follow-up work. Gingold heard from students that encouragement to stretch their bodies opposite the usual crouched posture, and rather, backward with "open wings," was refreshing and helpful.

Without the usual passing periods and recess breaks of school, many students benefited from encouragement to set limits on their screen time, to take breaks from schoolwork, and to get outside. Also, video conferences that had only informal social goals, rather than academic goals, allowed students to connect with each other. SEL practitioners can help teachers build in break times and offer appropriate unstructured time on video chat that still engenders some of the SEL that may be easier or more informal in person.

Teachers' Social-Emotional Health

In coding responses on the survey of teachers, Potter noticed a great deal of alignment between her own on-the-ground experience and the concerns that teachers expressed in the qualitative section. These emotional patterns held largely true for teachers at independent schools as well.

Teachers often expressed a feeling of powerlessness that stemmed from being overwhelmed by suddenly finding themselves in a new teaching environment. Because of the lack of overall preparedness for situations such as these, teachers found themselves coaching families one by one through the use of online tools. For teachers in large districts, this was exacerbated by the difficulty in getting a hold of families. Perhaps this meant the family was busy but faring well, or were they perhaps in too much emotional distress to respond? This unanswered question was an additional stressor on a teacher's deeply held sense of responsibility to their students.

Many teachers have children of their own, putting them in a position of managing the new learning environment at both ends—remote teaching and the family learning unit. At the same time, some teachers confided that, as much as families had found new ways to pause and appreciate time together, they also appreciated not having an early commute and enjoying the ability to control their work environment in ways they could not have if they were teaching on campus.

It's Okay Not to Be Okay

Gingold notes that teachers themselves have different levels of social-emotional skill. She made it part of her work to identify emotionally intelligent teachers who could help her connect with students of concern, even if they were not designated as that student's advisor. Since a trusted adult is key to a student's sense of social-emotional belonging, this strategy ensured that Gingold could find a way into the emotional life of any student.

With their natural impulse to focus on the needs of others, teachers can sometimes forget to consciously prioritize their own social-emotional health. "I think we're scared to be seen as less than perfect for kids," says Williams. "I don't think that people took a step back and said, *What is it that I need as an adult, so that I can then be here for kids?*" She also emphasizes that a teacher's humanity can be a stabilizing influence for students, or at least offer them some perspective on a pandemic compounded by a national race crisis. "I found the greatest power in saying to the kids *No, I'm not okay, because the pandemic is not normal. The amount of death that surrounds us now is not normal. And it's okay not to be okay.*" Since much of social-emotional learning is modeling by adults, students can begin to understand that vulnerability and strength are not mutually exclusive. In Gingold's words, "We all have life dilemmas and uncomfortable states. That's part of being human. Emotion itself is not necessarily the problem; it's what we do with it."

Ironically, the time away from school often had the effect of fostering gratitude in students. Not only did students become more consciously grateful for their teachers and friends, Potter notes, but also families were forced to slow down and reconsider what was really important to them. She said that many realized that they were doing too many things, and that cutting back might actually benefit the social-emotional health of the entire family in that "…we really value time just *being* together, and not necessarily *doing* things together."

Summary

Mr. Delavan did independent research for this chapter, conducting interviews and synthesizing current SEL thinking in education. Social Emotional health planning will arm schools with important tools to help teachers, students, and parents face crises.

Resources

Institute for Social and Emotional Learning
https://www.instituteforsel.net

Yale Center for Emotional Intelligence
https://www.ycei.org

Collaborative for Academic, Social, and Emotional Learning
https://casel.org

Carol Dweck's *Mindset*
https://www.penguinrandomhouse.com/books/44330/mindset-by-carol-s-dweck-phd/

The Pandemic's Toll on Children With Special Needs and Their Parents
https://www.nytimes.com/2020/07/27/well/family/children-special-needs-pandemic.html

Forefront Suicide Prevention
https://intheforefront.org

The Trevor Project – supporting LGBTQ Youth with Suicide Hotline
http://www.thetrevorproject.org

Minnesota PK-12 Distance Learning Survey
https://www.cehd.umn.edu/research/distance-learning/

> ▶ **School Leadership Committee Takeaway**
> Most schools tended to the social-emotional needs of stakeholders when COVID-19 closed schools everywhere.
> - How did you check on the social-emotional health of teachers, students, parents, and fellow administrators when school was closed?
> - Do you have an SEL program in place currently?
>   - If so, how did your assumptions and program perform during this crisis?
>   - If not, are you considering putting SEL in place?
>   - What will that look like?
>   - Who will be trained, and how?
>   - How will the curriculum be adjusted?
>   - How will students be involved – not just as targets of the learning, but as prime stakeholders?
>   - Will you use any of the programs described in this chapter?

- Do you survey your stakeholders for SEL regularly?
  - If so, were you able to compare results from a previous year with your March 2020 to the beginning of the school year results?
  - If not, will you begin surveying by stakeholders (teacher, parents, student, admin, staff)?
    - Who will conduct the surveys, and how?
    - Who will evaluate the results, and how?
    - Will you find themes that will be tied to specific programs for 2020-21 and beyond?

Chapter 4 – Leadership

Introduction

Leadership of any organization is key to success, and COVID-19 has amplified this need. I immediately thought of one person with the knowledge, skill, and understanding to write on leadership: Dr. Scott McLeod. Dr. McLeod was also interviewing educators on his highly-recommended podcast, *Coronavirus Chronicles* (http://dangerouslyirrelevant.org/tag/coronavirus-chronicles).[9] I'd collaborated with Dr. McLeod in the past, so I reached out and I'm pleased to say he agreed to write this chapter.

Leadership in Times of Crisis

Over the past few months, I have had two experiences which have greatly shaped my understandings related to leadership behaviors and support structures during times of crisis. First, in late March, I started interviewing school leaders around the globe about their individual and organizational responses during the coronavirus pandemic. Second, I taught a special topics course this summer at my university titled *Leadership During a Crisis*. My conversations with leaders across multiple organizations have been incredibly illuminating. In this chapter, I share some key insights and highlights from what I have learned.

---

[9] McLeod, Scott. Dangerously ! Irrelevant. *Coronavirus Chronicles*. various dates. accessed August 1, 2020.

Coronavirus Chronicles Interviews

Since March 2020, I have spoken with dozens of different educational organizations across the United States for my ongoing *Coronavirus Chronicles* interview series. I also have interviewed school leaders in China, Italy, Saudi Arabia, Luxembourg, Thailand, The Netherlands, Canada, Ecuador, and Tanzania. At the time I write this chapter, I have conducted a total of 43 interviews, all of which are available on my blog, *Dangerously Irrelevant*. My goals have been to hear first-hand how schools are responding during this unprecedented worldwide challenge, and to try and distill some essential lessons about how to lead during a time of crisis.

Figure 1. School responses to the COVID-19 pandemic

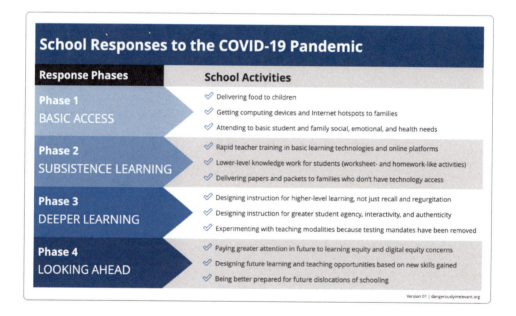

School Responses: Phases 1 and 2

The chart in Figure 1 is a distillation of my meaning-making from these interviews. What I heard first, of course, was the dreadful toll that the pandemic had on local schools and families. Communities everywhere struggled to keep children fed and citizens healthy. For instance, school districts found numerous creative ways to deliver breakfast and lunch to low-income children, sometimes even to students in nearby neighborhoods that weren't theirs. As one administrator said, "almost everyone participates. We accept anyone under the age of 18 that comes through our drive-through and picks up food, so it doesn't even matter if they're part of the school system or not." Another said, "buses essentially became mobile food wagons . . . they supplied six days' worth of food for every family that showed up [at the bus stop]."

Schools also did their utmost to check in with every single child and family to see what their medical, health, educational, and emotional needs were, and then connect them to appropriate resources. Those efforts often were both heroic and dismaying, particularly as they simultaneously tried to cope with the loss of loved ones. As one educator noted, "The sheriff just reported that although overall crime has dropped about 15%, the crimes of domestic abuse and child abuse have gone up close to 30%. . . . All of our counselors and teachers have set up into teams, and we're just constantly contacting kids, making sure we get them all in." All of these activities are summarized in Phase 1 of the chart above.

In addition to being an inspiration, local schooling also often turned out to be a challenge. While we saw daily examples of educators and school systems doing amazing things on behalf of children and parents, many of our schools also realized that previous under-investments in digital technologies, professional learning, and crisis preparedness resulted in critical delays or deficiencies regarding remote learning and teaching. This was particularly apparent in the second phase of most schools' responses.

If schools focused on basic survival needs during Phase 1, during Phase 2 they started to focus on what I am calling 'subsistence learning,' which is basically low-level knowledge work that students typically do with worksheets and for homework. This kind of learning dominated because it was the easiest to distribute quickly. For families that did not have computing devices or Internet access at home, schools tried to get paper packets home to families in order to keep this type of learning moving along. They also trained teachers with technology as fast as they could to try and remedy digital pedagogy skill gaps. For most schools and families, subsistence learning was the best they could manage over the past few months, and they often struggled mightily to serve children with special needs or linguistic concerns.

School Responses: Phases 3 and 4

The two phases just described probably feel familiar to those of us who are educators and parents. They describe the reality of basic survival for most schools and focus on the abrupt transition needs that we have seen during the pandemic crisis. There are two other phases in the chart, however, and I encourage all of us as educators and school leaders to try and focus on these in the months and years to come, especially if we continue to vacillate between face-to-face, online, and blended learning modalities for students.

During Phase 3, schools emerge from basic survival mode and start to think about richer, deeper learning opportunities for students. They also may see that this is a time during which they might experiment, because testing and accountability mandates may have been removed by state and national governments. Students deserve more from schools than factual recall and procedural regurgitation, even during 'remote emergency instruction.' Some schools I interviewed tried new ways of giving students more agency over their own learning, and they began to provide students some opportunities to engage in those 'deeper learning' opportunities that we know our graduates need for life success in a global innovation society. One school I interviewed continued to deploy a full International Baccalaureate program remotely. Another instituted 'iChoose Tuesdays,' a day full of at-home challenges in which students could engage in baking, STEM, fine arts, poetry, short story, and other projects. Yet another noted that their previous capacity-building in student-directed learning and competency-based progressions made their transition much easier than for many other schools.

Again and again, I heard from school leaders that if they were already oriented toward 'future-ready' learning and teaching modalities, they were able to adapt more quickly and easily than their more traditional counterparts. Distributed leadership structures that allowed educators to be flexible, adaptive decision-makers were key. So were problem- and inquiry-based instructional designs in which students were comfortable and ready to lead their own learning. One high school principal described their adaptation as follows:

> We initially were going to reach out to some of our mentors and ask the question, "Are there still opportunities for our students right now?" And of course, we realized very quickly as everything was disintegrating, this was not the time for us to reach out to our partners but instead to show them grace and allow them to figure out their own needs. So instead, what we did as a staff was we developed a personal project that asked our students to focus on one of four domains: a personal interest that you've never really had the time to develop; a skill from a loved one or a family member you've always wanted to learn but have never had time to learn; an online base skill, perhaps from a free open source website that you've always wanted to learn, maybe there's a way for you to learn that; and then the fourth one was something creative outside of your comfort zone. Do you want to make something? Do you want to build something?
>
> One of my advisees decided to build owl boxes out of some used wood that was in her father's garage. So the question was simply, "How are you going to challenge yourself and - even if it's not necessarily toward your personal career trajectory - what is something that's going to fill you up and is going to challenge you?" And we had our students take those projects on with gusto. The other gift that I think the coronavirus time has offered us is how well this illustrated that meaningful, inquiry-based learning that is connected to students' passions would create interest regardless of a grade.

That last idea is so powerful: meaningful, inquiry-based learning that creates student interest and passion regardless of a grade. This is the kind of instructional leadership our students and families deserve from every school, whether we're remote during a pandemic or in a more traditional face-to-face classroom setting.

Equity Issues

Phase 4 is equally important. During the summer, we had a chance to look back and plan forward. While much was unknown about what schooling would look like in Fall 2020, there still was a great deal that could be worked on. Some leaders and school systems did so, and for others, it's never too late. It's always a good time to pay greater attention to equity concerns, particularly around food and housing insecurity, instruction for students with special needs, and basic digital access. As learning and teaching moved online during the pandemic, many schools wished that every child had a computing device at home, so it's time to revisit our need to provide a take-home computer for every K-12 child. Many schools discovered that home Internet access for their students wasn't what they thought, so now is a good time to work with community partners to ensure greater connectedness for low-income families. Particularly as we operate in schooling contexts in which perhaps half of our students are in our buildings and the other half are at home, we need to begin thinking about how to restructure our classrooms and curricula and help educators learn how to live safely and teach powerfully in hybrid or 'hyflex' https://edtechbooks.org/hyflex[10] teaching modalities rather than wholly online or entirely face-to-face. Now is a great time to discuss how to shift our online and hybrid learning toward deeper, richer learning opportunities for our children. Now is also a fantastic time to talk with our workforce partners about how better to transition experiential learning like Career and Technical Education, community-embedded service- and project-based learning, and senior capstones into online or blended opportunities.

---

10 Beatty, Brian J. edtechbooks.org/hyflex. Hybrid-Flexible Course Design. n.d. accessed August 15, 2020.

Special Topics Course: *Leadership During a Crisis*

In addition to talking with school leaders across the planet, I also had the wonderful opportunity this summer to teach a special topics course on crisis leadership. It was a phenomenal learning experience for all of us, primarily because my students co-constructed the course with me. In addition to engaging with a variety of readings, podcasts, and videos that my students helped select, we decided to invite leaders from numerous societal sectors to talk with us. Over the course of the summer, we spoke with leaders in P-12 and higher education, business, the fine arts, and the hospitality industry. We talked with fire chiefs and military leaders, and we spoke with someone who runs the COVID floor at a hospital in Denver. As you can imagine, thinking about the actions and mindsets of leaders in fields outside of education was both fascinating and informative for us as educators.

Over and over again, we heard across all societal sectors about the importance of leading with personal and organizational values. As one of our guests noted, during times of crisis in which traditional decision-making pathways become uncertain, "our core values are the only thing to guide us in the dark." Whether the organization is a hotel or hospital or school in which the needs of the 'clients' are first and foremost, values-driven leadership allows for flexibility while remaining true to institutional mission and purpose. As our hospitality industry leader reminded us, "Mission, vision, and values are enduring, while the strategies and techniques necessary to accomplish those are context-specific." Effective leaders and organizations know how to shift strategies as necessary without compromising institutional goals and values.

We also heard from every leader about the importance of identifying a few key focal areas for action and then relentlessly messaging around them. Leaders who were able to clearly articulate three to five primary action steps or goals for their organizations could then incorporate numerous smaller activities by their employees under those larger umbrellas, reminding staff repeatedly that "the reason we're doing this is because it helps us accomplish one of our primary objectives during this difficult time." Our leadership guests also noted that when everything is changing constantly, there is a temptation to compare yourselves - or allow others to compare you - to what other schools or districts are doing. However, effective leaders do what's necessary and appropriate for their organizations and communities, planning for their needs rather than being reactionary to the activities of others.

Another theme we heard from our course guests was the necessity of raw honesty in order to retain trust. Successful leaders don't sugarcoat challenges, nor do they ignore the internal organizational deficiencies that may make those issues difficult to address. In other words, even if an organization was ill-equipped internally to deal with the crisis, noting that lack of readiness, outlining steps that were being taken to increase institutional capacity, and communicating to staff a positive outlook on the situation were all avenues for a successful outcome. In contrast, leaders that ignore their organization's lack of preparation, underinvest in institutional capacity-building, or pretend that everything is just fine are not able to respond in needed directions when crises happen. This requires prior organizational cohesiveness through teambuilding and trust-building. Our leadership guests noted repeatedly that fostering trust across the organization was something that needed to happen beforehand in order for them to then lead effectively during the crisis.

All of the leaders we met with also noted that it was absolutely critical to diminish organizational risk aversion during a crisis. Stated another way, every successful leader - whether on a military patrol in Iraq, fighting a wildfire in California, or adjusting during a pandemic - found ways to make it safe for their employees to try new things and fail forward. As one P-12 leader stated after getting blanket approval from his school board for a wide slate of actions, "We don't have time with the board to deal with votes and contract approvals. We need to move now. Children and families will suffer." He also said to his educators, "We're going to fail, perhaps miserably, over and over again [in this new environment], but that does not relieve us of our responsibility. You will not be reprimanded or fired if you're willing to lean in and begin adapting your practice." Similarly, our military guest noted the importance of organizational bricolage https://

papers.ssrn.com/sol3/papers.cfm?abstract_id=882784[11] - being able to create from a wide variety of possible options - and employees being bricoleurs, able to adapt rapidly and evolve using whatever's available to them. Many educators felt completely lost during the recent pandemic because there was no prior training for the type of crisis that occurred. However, hospital floors, fire crews, and military departments train repeatedly not just for expected events but also for the unexpected through diverse scenario planning. This prior investment pays off when new challenges arise suddenly.

Finally, and perhaps counterintuitively, our leadership guests reminded us that there are times to lead, and there are times to step back and be a follower. While it's important for everyone to understand their piece of the problem, leaders do not always have to be the ones out in front. If other employees in the organization have better ideas or skills for a particular challenge, good leaders give those individuals the authority, responsibility, and support necessary to lead the way. As one of our higher education leaders noted, "You don't always have all the answers, and that is okay. Ask for authentic input, co-construct with others, and let them lead with you." Too often, leaders' egos get in the way of more effective responses during crisis situations because they feel that they have to be the ones that own all of the solutions. Effective leaders are not diminished by handing over control and power to others in the organization who are better suited to address a particular concern.

Conclusion

One of the things we should recognize from the past few months is that the pandemic jolted many of us into acquiring some new mindsets and skillsets, whether we wanted to or not. For instance, many educators now have new technological and pedagogical capabilities that they didn't have before. They were forced by necessity to acquire them quickly, and many have discovered that incorporating some basic technology tools into their instruction wasn't as

---

11 E Cunha, Miguel Pina. SSRN. *Bricolage in Organizations.* FEUNL Working Paper No. 474. February 19, 2006. retrieved September 1, 2020.

difficult as they may have thought. Many of us also have realized that some of what we considered critical before faded away during the crisis. We had to distill our curricular content and our instructional approaches to their essence, focusing instead on the most essential learning, relationships, better communication with families, enhanced academic support structures, and taking care of each other.

Perhaps most importantly, many teachers and administrators also have new understandings about the speed of potential educational change and what we can accomplish in a short period of time if we put our minds to it. We no longer can say 'we can't do that' because we just did it, right? Savvy school leaders will begin to create organizational structures that allow staff to reflect deeply on the ways in which they were able to change quickly and then capitalize on those to keep moving the institution forward in needed directions.

For those of you who are familiar with Maslow's Hierarchy of Needs, the chart introduced at the beginning of the chapter is basically an organizational resemblance of that framework. As we think about the schools that we serve, we should try and recognize what phases they are in and why they are there. Reflection on the 'why' is actually the most important part. School administrators and board members need to be able to critically dissect why some educators in their organizations were more successful than others, and why some schools were more successful than others as well. Numerous differences in leadership behaviors, support structures, and instructional capacity exist across schools and classrooms. If we are to be prepared for whatever crisis comes next, our school systems will need to be thoughtful, reflective, and savvy diagnosticians.

Schools also will need to lean heavily into the challenge of putting plans and structures into place that allow them to move out of whatever phases they currently are in and into schooling modalities that are more than mere subsistence learning. Despite the pandemic, in a complex world, we still need our graduates to be critical thinkers and problem-solvers, not just regurgitators. We also need our educators to embrace risks, try new things, and share ownership for institutional challenges instead of just being rule-followers. Creating new organizational behaviors and belief systems will allow schools to move beyond compliance, adopt more robust mindsets around what's possible, and ultimately become much more resilient and adaptive.

Unfortunately, the pandemic exposed a number of critical leadership and organizational gaps that we should have paid greater attention to earlier. As a result, some school systems are more ready than others to adapt to the current crisis - or the next one. For example, some schools have invested heavily in educators' ability to implement high-quality, high-engagement online, or blended learning, while others engaged in magical thinking that they would reopen as normal. Some schools found ways to mobilize their communities and garner resources to close family equity gaps regarding computing devices and Internet access, while others simply crossed their fingers and hoped that the government would do something on that front. Some school leaders had brave conversations, gathered allies, and communicated realistically, frequently, and coherently to their communities, while others dithered. And so on...

As the saying goes, 'never waste a good crisis.' Now is the time for us to lean into those conversations and initiate action in neglected areas. As our fire chief guest told us, "Firefighters are trained to walk with purpose toward an emergency. They never run because the margin for error increases exponentially. This allows them to survey the scene and make thoughtful decisions while still acting decisively." Walking forward with purpose is fantastic advice for all of us as school leaders. Along with our community partners, let's launch some necessary changes in how we educate and serve our children and families. That would turn this terrible pandemic into a 'silver lining' for education and is a worthy goal for all of us.

Dr. Scott McLeod is an Associate Professor of Educational Leadership at the University of Colorado Denver and the Founding Director of the UCEA Center for the Advanced Study of Technology Leadership in Education (CASTLE). He can be reached at dangerouslyirrelevant.org or @mcleod on Twitter.

▶ **School Leadership Committee Takeaway**
- Is leadership in your school shared or centralized?
  - How and who assumes leadership for your stakeholders – teachers, students, parents, administrators?
    - Are there leadership assumptions inherent in these groups? If so, what are these assumptions?
    - Were there any leaders who "stepped up" when school was closed? Who and how?
      - Can they be part of your committee or report what went well, and what was challenging?
- Is leadership taught as a discipline in your school? If so, how might this unusual time be represented in that course or program?
- Are your school leaders assessed in the form of a survey or another vehicle?
  - Will you do a post COVID closing assessment?
- How was leadership different during school closing?
- How was leadership similar to the day-to-day running of the school or specific departments or functions?
- What would be your school leadership TED Talk as a result of the school closing?
  - Who or what groups might give the talk?

Chapter 5 – Relationships

Introduction
Learning is Social – Relationships are Its Currency

We know from research and educators' experience that learning is socially constructed and requires a relationship between the learner and the teacher. We are social creatures, and education is also social. Vygotsky's work regarding Sociocultural Theory, which describes how learning is social, is widely accepted by educators.

Given the premise that learning is social, then relationships are its currency. Social interactions happen within relationships. We learn about one another through our conversations, shared activities, and body language. We find out others' values, philosophies, humor, perspective, culture, needs, expectations, preferences, political views, strengths, challenges, and beliefs. All of these observations and impressions combine to create the relationship between two or more people.

Effective teachers work hard to build strong relationships with their students. They seek to understand what makes each child unique. Most teachers describe their students using insight based on their observations of and interactions with children. Observation is a crucial assessment tool that teachers use to learn about their students.

Students, too, are continually absorbing information and developing impressions about teachers. They notice how teachers teach, how they speak to other students, and how they react to questions or challenges. Students develop relationships with their teachers based on their interpretation of those factors.

Parents also form relationships with teachers. They will meet with teachers during back-to-school night, parent conferences, and other school events. Parents will interact through phone calls or email exchanges with teachers. The relationship between teacher and parent is an important one; teachers must work to ensure that communication is compelling so that that parents can support the efforts the teacher is making in the classroom.

Contributor Michelle Back provides an eye-opening glimpse at life as a parent with small school age children during the pandemic.

Non-verbal and verbal communication, even when we are not paying attention, is the subtle and actual contributor to all our relationships.

Teachers and Students

The currency of a relationship, the give and take, the deepening of the teacher-to-student relationship happens in the classroom when students and teachers are in the same space at the same time. The classroom becomes the vehicle for instruction with the teacher outlining expectations, coaching and mentoring students, and fostering progress.

Other things happen in the classroom. Teachable moments can occur when a student brings up an idea that veers to an interesting subtopic. A spontaneous event or joke may cause everyone to laugh. Changes to the daily schedule might require teachers and students to depart from the routine. There can be internal or external classroom surprises, both positive and negative.

When school buildings were closed during the pandemic, the common elements from the school disappeared. These elements included rooms, libraries, study halls, cafeterias, whiteboards, classroom computers, and even desks and chairs. Time, space, and objects in schools were part of the flow and experience of life in school. All these elements were no longer available when learning moved to homes.

Remote Learning Makes Relationships Different With Students

Remote learning through technology or even without technology is different socially. Synchronous and asynchronous learning requires screens. Cameras for synchronous learning change the experience of a student-teacher relationship. It takes time for the camera to "disappear" for students and teachers, and not be the focus.

Most teachers before COVID-19 did not have professional development for online instruction. Many teachers were not familiar with video conferencing tools. Well-planned lessons and units had to be adjusted or revamped to be delivered online.

Relationships online became different when classroom elements were gone. Teachers no longer had control over time and space.

"... faculty recognize that a lot of the casual relationship building that happens during class time becomes difficult virtually."- James Bologna

"We can't see them physically; it's a big change in day-to-day interaction. (Teachers) couldn't live in the moment in the same way, especially to non-verbal cues - with spontaneous light jokes, relationships, connections, redirects, and impactful lesson tangents." – Patrick Hausammann

Teachers Who had Relationships with Students Found More Success

Schools closed in March 2020 all around the world. It was one thing for teachers who knew and had relationships with most of their students. But teachers who didn't know their students well had difficulty engaging with them when physical presence was not possible. Forming relationships during remote emergency learning proved to be difficult, although not impossible.

"Teachers who worked hard to build relationships will be most effective ... if you didn't know students before, it's a lot harder to get to know them near the end of the

school year. Kids without relationships with the teacher have the lowest return rate of assignments and projects."

> Tara Johanneson
> Technology integrationist and teacher
> Bishop O'Gorman Catholica Schools, Sioux Falls SD

"Teachers are "seeing students in a different light than in the classroom. ... teachers are actively reaching out to students, seeing more of their environment to help them ... but if teachers don't have a relationship with a student, the trust isn't there." – Arline Pique

Remote learning is not brand new, however. There are charter and cyber schools that have been teaching students online for some time; even students never meet in person. Higher education has been offering online and blended learning courses and has found ways to engage students that can be changed and applied to 6-12 students.

Students and Teachers Miss Each Other

Many interviewees reported that students and teachers alike were missing each other. Students wanted to be in school and to see teachers and other students. Teachers missed their students and were worried about them. The day-to-day connection, which seemed mundane in the pre-pandemic time, became valuable once it was not available.

"One of the biggest feedbacks we have received from our students is how much they miss their teachers and school staff." – Todd Wesley

Some teachers organized "drive-by" caravans in neighborhoods where their students lived, sometimes in decorated cars. Students stood in front of their homes and waved to teachers. Sometimes teachers were able to visit students and talk behind windows. Of course, this depended on the school and the teachers. Visiting was not always possible in urban or remote school districts.

Other teachers found ways to acknowledge that they were all missed and form new experiences with students online. Social-emotional health needed to be at the forefront of the brand new remote relationships between students and teachers. Feelings were often freely shared.

Teachers and Students in Each Other's Homes

Synchronous remote learning meant video conferencing. Cameras on for video sessions showed rooms where students or teachers lived, along with the furniture and surroundings. It sometimes meant a teacher's home with their spouse or partner, pets, and children in view.

"Teachers are getting a more personal view of the kids and their learning process and the rhythm of life. They're now in your living or dining room." - Jason Curtis

"Instructionally, our teachers have shown grace and expanded understanding that home situations are not equal, and remote learning has its own benefits and challenges, so learning expectations must shift." - Todd Wesley

Issues of equity and privacy occurred. Cameras brought students' living situations into view; some students had more expensive homes than others. Sometimes other children or adults were moving in and out of sight. Teachers and schools needed to be sensitive about this. Teachers previously controlled the space, time, and environment when they taught in school building spaces. Controlling factors such as the environment was not possible with remote learning.

Compassion and understanding need to be shared freely around issues of equity. Teachers may want to start with 1-on-1 video sessions and reach out to parents before adding other students to live meetings.

Establishing protocols for video sessions can be helpful. Equity should not be a factor when video conferencing into a student or teacher's home. Parents should be involved so they can be aware of any concerns.

Students Who Didn't Participate Before Still Didn't

Some students don't participate in class or turn in homework and are frequently absent. Teachers continually reach out to these students to get them involved. Interviewees said the same thing happened with remote learning. Changing the mode of instruction does not magically alter the dynamics with students.

Sometimes students "ghosted" – they were unreachable and did not show up for synchronous sessions, nor did they respond to emails or other communications from the teacher.

"Teachers echoed the same thing; they are still chasing kid; they chased in person, just online –it hasn't changed. "– Milena Streen

When a child is not participating or is unreachable, most schools will involve school counselors, principals, or other staff to reach out to parents. Remote learning also used school counselors and staff to contact parents. Contact becomes complex when no one is in a physical school.

Helping Students "Get It" When Online

Teachers have many techniques in the classroom to see which students are "getting it," and to reach those who are not. They learn what works with their students. But when they are not in the same space as the children they teach, new techniques are needed.

Teachers still guide students through concepts with remote instruction. Successful teaching online requires new approaches.

Professional development geared towards remote learning is a significant need for all schools. Helping teachers become adept in this teaching environment is crucial. Chapter 7 provides useful ideas for online learning from a current professional development coach and teacher.

Recommendations

- Build on the existing classroom relationships and find ways to amplify what the physical classroom offers;
- Use virtual video backgrounds, participate in spirit days with students dressing according to a theme, or sharing something in their home that relates to a topic;
- Have students brainstorm ideas individually or in groups to make virtual learning more fun;
- Find ways for students to help design and improve the remote learning environment;
- Use breakout rooms and have students work on projects in groups;
- Explore music, videos, and other media to engage students;
- Use video conference platforms for 1-on-1 meetings with students, meetings with groups of students, and whole-class instruction;
- Combat video conferencing "fatigue" by teacher and student by developing a more flexible schedule;
- Establish online video etiquette and involve students and parents;
  - Topics can include where to connect, how to be dressed, the use of cameras, establishing a quiet background, informing the family there will be video conferencing;
- Prepare teachers for having students "in their homes," and how to deal with surprises; Teachers may have the first session with individual students to share best practices and anticipate any problems;
- Protect the privacy of students including whether they should see each other's homes;

- Involve teachers in a "postmortem" exercise based on the coronavirus pandemic and gather best practices and cautionary tales to inform your School Remote Learning Plan;
- Make sure teachers have technical and emotional support all day, every day during remote emergency learning;
- Provide both drop-in times (to ask anything) and remote skills professional development for teachers;
- Support Teacher-to-teacher communication as fluid and frequent either through your LMS, "happy hour" video times, or during scheduled support times;
- Encourage teachers to share, collaborate, and commiserate for their social-emotional health and to support students;
- Involve counselors as needed for social-emotional health struggles;
- Share technical support contact information with teachers;
- Contact parents as needed;
- Expect more parents to be reaching out, so consider scheduling video parent hours and sharing FAQs with parents who cannot attend.

Teacher and Parent Relationships

When remote emergency learning happens suddenly, it can impact parents as well. For COVID-19, many parents had to work from home or found themselves unemployed overnight. Employment in the U.S. remains precarious as of the writing of this book. Teachers found that their relationships with parents changed when parents were home with children during the school day.

Parents observed firsthand how their children work with teachers. They were able to see struggles and challenges up close. Parents gained insight when they witnessed their children learning. Parents watched how their child responded positively and negatively to instruction, which sometimes led to support and encouragement at home.

- **Author Anecdote**

I recall working at a school where a child was struggling. The teachers had told the parents and tried to explain what they observed, but the parents did not grasp what was going on and initially weren't supportive. One day the parents were invited to sit in the back of the class and observe their son. Instead of participating verbally or watching the lesson unfold, he doodled continually, not responding to the teacher's prompts and not taking notes. Once the parents observed their son's actual behavior in the classroom, parents were able to fully support the school's recommendation for the child's instruction.

It was invaluable for those parents to get first-hand insight by being in their son's classroom. Most parents have never had the opportunity to see their child learning during the school day – until this pandemic.

"Parents are with their students at home and starting to understand struggles in the classroom."- Arline Pique

Suddenly a Parent-Teacher-Student Conversation

Remote emergency learning during the coronavirus pandemic meant many parents were home either working or unemployed. Parents were near their children while instruction took place, sometimes close enough to participate in video meetings. Having parents nearby changed the teaching dynamic, which made teachers adjust to having a new participant. Teachers gained different relationships with parents, becoming closer partners in many instances.

"… this was a parent-teacher-student conversation. The parent was close enough to join the conversation. It changed things." - James Bologna

"Today, teachers, parents, and students are meeting all day in their student conferences. Sometimes they have a laugh. Parents understand what their child is doing in class

and are truly appreciative and supportive of the learning environment the teacher has created for their child." - Mario Fishery

The demands of the classroom day used to mean that teachers contacted parents after hours when both were available. Teachers and parents weren't available for conversations and reports on learning progress when schools were open.

Some parents remained unavailable during the school day because of their jobs. It varied from family to family, whether teachers and parents could speak during the day. Teachers still had long days.

Parents Understand Teacher's Role

Seeing with your own eyes how hard teachers work and the art of instruction caused parents' understanding of teaching to shift. The subtle interactions and the complex activities, the actions and reactions, the intricate dance between the teacher and student were always fascinating to watch. Many parents have not been in a classroom since they were students. They were unaware of current instructional methods. Seeing teaching and learning unfold in front of them with their children as students opened their eyes.

"… a lot of parents have a new respect for teachers."

> *Mike Daugherty*
> *Director of Technology & Innovation*
> *Chagrin Falls Exempted Village Schools, Chagrin Falls OH*

"… [The] teachers' position and roles are going to be more understood and respected by students and parents. This became a great opportunity to build the parent-teacher relationship and build more of a school-home collaboration going forward." - Tara Johanneson

There has been a pushback by some parents towards teachers and teaching since the interviews. Many are encouraging schools to reopen even though some teachers fear for their and their students' health. Once businesses and organizations started opening up, and parents returned to physical places of work, parents began worrying about what would happen when schools opened back up. Parents were used to having their children in school while they worked.

No one comes out ahead when a global pandemic pits different stakeholders against each other.

My strong feeling is that health and safety are always first.

The Volume of Communication Increased

During this emergency, parents wanted to be informed. They reached out to teachers and others to see how the crisis impacted their child or children. They tried to understand the school or district's short- and long-term plans. Expectations of parents and students were unclear.

"We're getting more community and parent communication" – Patrick Hausammann

"… more phone calls are being made. A lot more immediacy is needed now." – Milena Streen

School communication used email, postal mail to parent homes, and Web page announcements. The pandemic required more frequent messages from the school to families and teachers.

A Parent Shares - Background

A friend of mine here in Eastern Washington, Michelle Back, was writing a daily Facebook reflection on life as a parent of two school aged children during COVID-19. Like other friends, I found myself seeking the daily reflection filled with fun, photos, occasional chaos, and the reality of how everything upturned suddenly. I couldn't close my social media check without reading about the Backs. I asked Michelle to contribute a reflection, and she kindly obliged.

Toppled into Chaos

Michelle Back
Professional Editor and Writer

In mid-March 2020, our careful work-school-life balance toppled into chaos. My partner and I sat down with our 4- and 7-year olds and told them that we were all going to be staying home—we would be working from home and they would no longer be going to their classrooms. They learned the word "quarantine." They already knew of the coronavirus.

This new way of life had rippling implications on how we would now be managing work and school schedules. We were among the privileged and lucky families who could hunker down and make quarantine life work, albeit somewhat imperfectly. There were and still are pain points. Childcare and schooling—two elements that happened outside the walls of our house—needed to happen firmly within the confines of home. I was already working half time but had to reduce my schedule further to 20% time to make everything work. I'm grateful that that was an option for us. It appears it's going to be a long-term change.

The kids had questions. "How long will we be staying home?" the kids wanted to know. "Can we see our friends?" they asked. The answers were and still are "we don't know," and "you can see your friends virtually." Virtually immediately became how we work and do school and make life happen. We telework, tele-school, and telesocialize. Shopping is done online. The coronavirus pandemic cocooned our physical world, but we still need to do things, like school.

For my 7-year-old daughter, the 2019-2020 school year was her first time in public school, and she was so excited for a bigger school, bigger classroom experience. She's a social butterfly. Previously she attended a Montessori school, but for first grade, public school was the best thing to happen to her. Her first-grade teacher was amazing—engaged, creative, and kind. She encouraged parent-teacher communication. Prior to school closures, we had a solid relationship and were in regular contact regarding my daughter's progress and classroom needs. My daughter's teacher already used an app to post updates regarding the class, and we could use the app to privately message when needed, like when my daughter decided not to return from recess on time one day.

I credit the success of our online learning experience to the sturdy foundation laid prior to school closure. Within a few days of school closing, my daughter's teacher set up what we assumed would be a temporary distance learning plan and disseminated it through the app with which we were already familiar. Once it was clear we would finish the school year online, her teacher expanded the learning experience by posting assignments online with a new app and communicating about them through the familiar app. It was a streamlined system and the learning curve was low. We could work at our own pace, which was nice because even though our online learning experience was good, it was not without tears and frustrations, mostly between my daughter and myself.

When I reached out to my daughter's teacher to say we were struggling to learn from home (because Mom is a poor substitute teacher), she set up a biweekly Zoom meeting so she and my daughter could check in and practice reading. There was also a weekly class Zoom meeting so the entire class could see each other and socialize—they did an art project, played a word game, and had a virtual treasure hunt, among other activities. Eventually her teacher expanded the biweekly meetings to everyone in the class, broken up into two-person groups. My daughter had a virtual reading buddy classmate (who incidentally was the one classmate she wasn't allowed to sit next to in school because she and her buddy wouldn't stop talking, but I think her teacher knew that that was the person my daughter needed to stay excited for the reading group).

The strong relationships my daughter's teacher built with parents and students was apparent throughout the school year, but never as much as the last week of classes. Her teacher dropped off a goodie bag that had an activity for every day of the last week of school at each student's house. Each morning the entire class had a Zoom meeting to choose an activity for the day—rock painting, chalk art, bubble activities, and glow-stick glasses. We all posted pictures of our creations for everyone in the class to see. For the last day of class, her teacher gathered classroom and quarantine pictures from students and compiled an end-of-year slideshow and virtually handed out awards. It was a sweet and cozy way to end a school year that was anything but normal.

In the chaos of figuring out how to navigate a pandemic, online schooling ended up being the one thing that became a known and familiar constant. The open lines of communication among my daughter's teacher, the students, and the parents were the best I could have hoped for. For other parents I know, the experience was not as glowingly positive. In some cases, it was frustratingly negative. I'm forever grateful for the calm-in-the-storm schooling experience.

For my 4-year-old son, unfortunately, his preschool curriculum all but stopped when his school closed. There were no mechanisms in place to continue lessons through distance learning. He's 4, so the push to keep school going wasn't as strong as it was for my daughter, but it would have been nice for him to have an online classroom experience as well, especially since we've already signed up my daughter for virtual public school in the fall and are hoping to have the same opportunity for him.

Author note

Interviewees said parents understood what teachers really did for their children when parents had to help from home. Parents struggled, but many found a way to cope. We can't let this moment go without acknowledging how much parents had to adapt. We also can't ignore how having a steady source of income, and a home that allowed remote learning, enabled possibilities. Not every family could say the same.

Recommendations

- Prepare teachers and staff for increased communication from parents and decide who is the contact person and the preferred modes of communication

- Share this plan with parents, along with contact information and hours
- Anticipate that parent-teacher conferences may now become parent-student-teacher conferences (if they weren't before)
- Encourage teachers to establish norms with parents as well as with students during the instructional day
- Provide parents and teachers with technical support contact information
- Protect the privacy of students as needed; there may be times when the teacher does not want other students' parents participating in activities
- Provide parents with an expected video conferencing schedule to prevent surprises
- Know that parents may be reaching out to teachers during hours outside of the usual school day, set expectations with parents, and share with teachers
- Seize the opportunity for parents to gain an understanding of what teachers really do with a plan to foster parent communication, support the school/district's programs, and deepen parent partnerships
- Teachers and schools need to seize the moment when parents grasp what teaching means. Schools can solidify parent communication, amplify the stories unfolding of parent/teacher relationships, share the value of educational programs, and bring parents more solidly into schools as partners. See Chapter 10 for more ideas on engaging with parents as part of your overall School Crisis Plan

Chapter 6 by Mike Daugherty shares more recommendations and advice.

▶ **School Leadership Committee Takeaway**
  - Educators interviewed mentioned relationships as integral to instructional success.

- How did relationships morph when school was closed?
- If you are starting up school only remotely, how will you address the need for relationships between teachers and students, teachers and parents, parents, and school leadership?
- How will the curriculum acknowledge and reinforce relationships during synchronous online instruction? During asynchronous online instruction?
- If you are using blended or hybrid learning, how will relationships be nurtured?

Chapter 6 – Communication

Introduction

When I interviewed Mike for the book, I was impressed with his knowledge and insight. Like other technology directors, he had to juggle resources, provide leadership, empower teachers, support parents, students, and teachers, and much more. He was an educator, a tech director, and a front-line leader as the crisis of the pandemic unfolded.

During the interview, Mike shared that he'd written a book, which I downloaded and enjoyed. I reached out to Mike to see if he might be interested in writing a chapter about communication, an essential element of leadership. I am pleased to say he agreed to do so.

Communication in the Time of a Crisis

> Mike Daugherty
> Director of Technology & Innovation
> Chagrin Falls Exempted Village Schools, Chagrin Falls OH

Communication Today

For the last one hundred and fifty years, communication has mostly been a one-way street. The school district carefully creates a message to be pushed out to the families, typically in the form of a physical letter mailed to the home address. Advances in technology have allowed districts to relay information through an email, a post on the district website, or an all call. These advances have increased the speed at which data is communicated, but the concept is still the same: Information is being passed from school to the family. This form of communication does not natively provide the person receiving the message with an opportunity to respond. A recipient can reply to the email or call the school, but neither of those avenues promotes conversation. This form of one way, top-down communication, is no longer acceptable.

The advent of text messaging and social media have changed the landscape of how schools should be communicating. We live in an on-demand society. We have developed a culture that relies on the pings, chirps and push notifications that comes with a stream of constant communication through a smartphone. The average person in America checks their smartphone 96 times per day. (Ausrion, 2019). https://www.prnewswire.com/news-releases/americans-check-their-phones-96-times-a-day-300962643.html[12] There is the expectation that a stakeholder will get information when they want it, in a format they prefer, on a platform where they spend most of their time connecting with others.

Organizations dedicated to advancing technology in education outline best practices for digital leaders. CoSN's Framework of Essential Skills for the K-12 CTO https://cosn.org/categories/it-management[13] includes an entire section devoted to communication. The framework stresses the importance of collaborating and communicating with district stakeholders on a consistent, ongoing basis. ISTE Standards for Educational Leaders www.iste.org/standards/for-education-leaders[14] address communication within three of the five standards: Visionary Planner, Systems Designer, and Connected Leader.

Communication with your district stakeholders during a crisis must embrace on-demand and conversation-driven concepts. What you say, when you say

12 CISION PR Newswire. *Americans Check Their Phones 96 Times a Day*. November 19, 2019. accessed June 1, 2020.
13 COSN. *Framework of Essential Skills*. n.d. accessed June 2, 2020.
14 ISTE. *ISTE Standards for Education Leaders*. n.d. accessed June 2, 2020.

it, and where you say it sets the stage either for panicked parents or controlled discussions. The messaging shapes the public's perception of how the district handled the event initially and in an ongoing way. A significant component of social-emotional health is knowing what is happening and how the changes will impact you. The value of thoughtful, well-worded communication cannot be understated. This chapter guides school leaders on how to effectively communicate with the community and with your team when it matters most.

Preparing

Let's look at a common scenario that occurs in school districts across the country. The superintendent sends an email to the entire school community providing an update on an important issue. Several social media posts are created on Twitter and Facebook, encouraging families to read the recently sent email. The information technology department inevitably receives emails from parents who are concerned because they did not receive the email. Every district has a process for gathering and updating the contact information for their families. Unfortunately, stakeholders will blame the district for lack of communication regardless of who is at fault for following that process. The perception will be that the district failed to keep parents informed. This unwanted perception will be magnified tenfold in a crisis.

The effectiveness of any communication campaign relies heavily on accurate contact information. In a perfect model, there would be one system responsible for collecting parent contact information. This one system would then push that contact information out to the variety of platforms used to communicate with stakeholders. The reality for most districts is that multiple systems collect overlapping data, and those systems do not always interact with each other. Accurate contact information is the result of three primary factors: software interoperability, human follow-up, and parent relationships.

Interoperability is the ability of two or more applications to pass information and instructions to one another. CoSN's Framework of Essential Skills for the K-12

CTO stresses the importance of interoperability when designing a communication system. An excellent example of interoperability is using the student information system (SIS) to provide phone numbers and email addresses to the district's all call system. When data is updated in the SIS, the all-call system receives that information in real-time or shortly after that. When the district chooses to send a communication, interoperability ensures the most current information is being used to direct delivery of that message. Current data is only as good as the accuracy of that information. What happens when the contact information is incorrect? You cannot expect to provide information to your families when you have outdated or inaccurate phone numbers and email addresses.

Checking for Human Error

The human interaction portion is the most flawed and most overlooked aspect of district communication preparation; however, it is the most important. Alexander Pope stated, "To err is human." The essence of that statement is that everyone makes mistakes. As someone who types his email address into various websites and applications no less than fifty times per pay, I still miss a letter once or twice a day. The point I am trying to make is that you cannot rely on your end users to enter accurate information. There has to be a system of checks and balances in place. The best way for this to occur is to have someone on the district staff read through the delivery reports from your various communication systems. For example, many schools use "Constant Contact" or "MailChimp" to send mass emails to their stakeholders. Every email campaign that is sent includes a bounce report of unsuccessful delivery attempts. This report will list the recipients who did not receive your message. Reaching the highest level of accuracy requires human interaction here. A staff member must be given the responsibility of reading through the bounce reports to determine where the error occurred and correct it. The same process should occur with the undeliverable reports generated by the all-call system. I believe this is often overlooked because correcting all of those mistakes may seem like a daunting task at first glance. The reality is that once the initial wave of errors is corrected, the maintenance of accurate information becomes much more manageable. Cleaning up incorrect data will pay dividends time and time again.

Parent relationships are another critical component of a district's communication plan. The district needs to set the expectations for where and when guardians and caregivers can expect to receive information. Using a consistent method of communication that aligns with expectations will build trust with your stakeholders. Additionally, parents must know where they can update their contact information when it changes.

A well-established system of communication should help prevent panic and misinformation in a crisis. The ideal system is a combination of technology used to perform the communication and a group of reliable, trustworthy individuals who can help spread the message. This would include formal and informal leaders in the community who support the district. Building this community of supporters is essential to effective communication, regardless of any crisis the schools may be facing.

The Association of Education Service Agencies has pre-written templates that can be used as a starting point. This sixteen-page document covers various crisis situations and offers sample texts to different stakeholder groups that can be edited as needed.

https://www.aesa.us/conferences/2015_ac_presentations/Handouts.pdf[15]

Communication to the Community

The crisis itself does not have as much of an impact on communication as one might think. Communication during a state or national emergency like the COVID-19 pandemic looks similar to communication during a localized crisis. Information is disseminated to districts in a national emergency, and leadership is responsible for communicating how this information will impact the schools. In a local disaster, such as a fire, or crisis, like a bomb threat, information is still being disseminated to district leaders from local police and fire officials.

---

15 AESA.US/conferences 2015/handouts. *Example Crisis Statements*. n.d. accessed June 3, 2020.

Communication still needs to include how this information impacts the school community. Excellent communication during a crisis relies heavily on what you say, when you say it, and where you say it.

These traits were present throughout the interviews conducted for this publication. Ms. Jennifer Fry said it best: *"The thing that I've been most proud about in our school district is that we worked collaboratively as a team and put forward consistent communications for teachers, community, and parents. We've really tried to have a plan the entire time."*

What You Say

Parents, the community, and the news media will be discussing, analyzing, and reading into your every word, so what you say is critical. You have built a level of trust with your community, and now, more than ever, honesty and transparency are the keys to success. Crisis communication should begin with the five Ws that most of us learned in grade school: Who, what, when, where, and why. The opening message should answer those five questions. This portion of the communication should describe the incident with as much honesty and transparency as the situation allows. The community will want to know what happened, when it happened, where it happened and who was involved. Answering the why can be difficult sometimes, depending upon the nature of the crisis. There will be times when holding back information will be necessary.

After the opening message, the next section should address what the district has done already, as well as what the next steps will be. Start with the district's response to the incident. For example, if a school experienced a gas leak, the text might read, "The safety and security of our students continue to be our primary concern. We immediately evacuated the building to a pre-identified location. District leaders contacted the local agencies (Police, Emergency Services, Health) to determine the appropriate course of action to ensure students received appropriate medical attention." Obviously, the exact nature of the incident will dictate the response. Once you've described how the district responded, it is important to explain the next steps in the process. The communication should address any necessary follow up activities.

Prior to concluding the text, detail any next steps that parents should take. This could include things such as scheduling a doctor's appointment if their child(ren) exhibits any symptoms or contacting the district if they have any information to share with leadership. This will vary hugely with each situation.

Close the letter with details on when parents can expect to hear more information. The next section, "When You Say It," discusses the frequency of communication and why knowing what to expect is essential.

When You Say It

Frequency is critical to effective communication. The trouble is finding a balance between too much and too little communication. Over-communicating can lead to important messages becoming lost in the shuffle. Under-communicating can lead to speculation and rumors on the part of your stakeholders. This is a common challenge that exists in most districts. The emotional panic induced by a crisis heightens people's need for answers. Emergencies and people's reactions to those emergencies are both unique and unpredictable. Unfortunately for district leaders, there is no leveled crisis rubric that indicates exactly when to reach out to your stakeholders.

It is important to send a message to the community once the immediate concern of the crisis has been addressed. The message should address various areas outlined above. Providing detailed communication about the situation, what was done, and what the next steps are will work to satisfy the social-emotional need for information along with easing fears generated by speculation and rumors. Close by is setting expectations for when people can expect additional information. The best strategy for frequency of communication in a crisis situation is keeping people informed of when additional information will be forthcoming. During the COVID-19 crisis, state governors began to have daily, scheduled press conferences to provide updated information. I believe many people took comfort in knowing there was a set schedule for these updates.

Where You Say It

The third focal point, where you say it, brings us back to the introduction of this chapter. District leadership must understand that stakeholders want both to hear from you and to be heard themselves. In order for stakeholders to hear you, it is essential to communicate with them in the places and platforms where they prefer to receive their communications. In layman's terms, to be heard, you need to meet people where they are. Your population of parents and caregivers will span from millennials to baby boomers. Posting your message to Facebook only reaches those individuals who actively use Facebook.

Similarly, an email only touches the stakeholders that use email regularly. Leadership must ensure messages are sent through a variety of platforms to ensure all stakeholders receive the communication. Peoples' enhanced emotional need for information during a crisis will increase the success of all avenues of communication; however, it is still incredibly important to use multiple channels. Important messages are often too long to convey in a tweet, text, or picture, however. Consider posting the primary information in a central location (like the website or a parent portal) and creating shorter posts on those other platforms that direct stakeholders to the primary message.

As previously stated, the one-way model of communication is not effective in our on-demand culture. Sending out an email, posting a message on the district website, or doing an all-call or broadcast call limits the stakeholders' ability to engage in a two-way conversation. Remember, in a crisis, individuals' emotions are heightened. They have questions, concerns, and strongly believe they need to be heard. Without a platform for that communication, people will seek out forums on social media to express their concerns. How many stories have you heard of where a spark on a community Facebook group starts a firestorm of misinformation that the district leadership struggles to contain? This is a common issue when people do not have a way to engage in a dialogue with the school. School districts should consider implementing a parent portal to address this problem. The portal is a place that is designed for parents to ask questions and voice their concerns in a way that allows trusted school administrators to respond. Messages sent to other platforms (Twitter, Instagram, Facebook, etc.) can direct parents to the portal. Parents and guardians will come to understand that the portal is the central location where all messages are shared, and questions are answered for all to see.

Follow Up

It is essential to gather feedback from your stakeholders once the crisis has subsided. The continuous improvement process includes a loop in which you gather feedback and then, based on that feedback, adjust your approach accordingly. The Visionary Planner standard from the ISTE standards for educational leaders references (International Society for Technology in Education, n.d.) the need to communicate effectively with stakeholders to gather input. You will want to know what you did effectively in your crisis communication, as well as what areas needed to be improved.

When surveying your stakeholders, keep the following design tips in mind:
- Build the survey in a way that allows you to see the data by stakeholder groups. For example, did the families with elementary children feel differently about your communication skills compared to families with older children?
- Ask a few families to take the survey and provide feedback prior to sending the survey to the entire school community. This can provide you with insight into how the survey is designed. It also provides you with some sample data to disaggregate. This ensures that the data you collect is going to be in a format that is easily analyzed.
- At least one question in the survey should revolve around the frequency of the communication. District leaders will want to know if the amount and frequency of communication was acceptable.

- One question should be a free response that allows stakeholders the opportunity to share their thoughts. A crisis situation evokes a lot of emotional response in individuals. Some people need the opportunity to express their feelings. Whether they want to thank you for your hard work or convey their anger, an open-ended response question is an excellent way to handle this desire.

Debrief Your Team

The final step in any crisis is to reflect on how your team handled the situation. We cannot expect to grow as leaders without assessing what we did well and where we faltered. The survey data should serve as a starting point for these discussions. Be prepared to have different perspectives and possibly some difficult conversations. Understanding the perception of your actions is almost as important as the actions themselves. Honesty will be the key to moving the team forward and preparing to deal with the next situation that arises.

Summary

Proficient leadership helps leaders guide communities through crises. Planning and effort around communication will be worth the time of school leadership.

> ▶ **School Leadership Committee Takeaway**
> - Thinking about the forms of communication used at your school when school was closed – what was the most effective? The least effective?
> - Have communication methods, frequency, and interactivity changed at your school over time? How?
> - Comparing communication during a crisis and a routine school year, what is the same? What is different?
> - Is communication centralized, with one person or group primarily communicating to your stakeholders, or decentralized with several people sending communication according to the content?

- Did the centralized vs. decentralized communication change in any way when school was closed?
  ○ What might you do differently in terms of communication in the future, based on how the school community reacted to the emergency school closing during COVID?

Chapter 7 –
Online Learning and Teachers

Introduction

This chapter begins with an explanation and results of a survey by Daniel Cruz and Megan Storey Hallam. Next is an excerpt of Lindy Hockenbary's well-written eBook on online learning. Following Lindy are some words from online expert Adrian Segar on learning using video tools. We end the contributors to this chapter with Michele Back, a parent providing her take on life facilitating online learning at home.

Teaching During COVID-19 Survey

Megan Storey Hallam
Director of Student Support Services
Nationally Certified School Psychologist
Léman Manhattan Preparatory School

Daniel Cruz
Educational Technology Coordinator
Léman Manhattan Preparatory School

COVID-19 Survey Introduction

As schools rapidly shifted to online learning in mid-March 2020, educator forums on social media were flooded with questions, concerns, and requests for assistance. While searching for answers ourselves, we quickly realized there was a need for the gathering and sharing of information for the benefit of teachers seeking to provide high-quality instruction and administrators tasked with leading schools through this crisis. During the week of March 20, 2020, we generated a list of recurring topics and questions from social media groups, blogs, and online educational publications. Next, we used thematic analysis of those topics to develop a survey focused on the transition to online learning, the main platforms for virtual teaching, and educator concerns, feelings of preparedness, and personal considerations.

Survey Results

A key finding of the survey was that 81% of respondents were expected to teach online during school closures, yet over 88% of participants reported that they did not have any experience in this area. Only 63% of teachers received training to prepare for virtual teaching, and the average length of training was 4.5 hours. Around 45% of the teachers surveyed indicated that they felt *somewhat prepared* to teach online, and 16% reported feeling *very well prepared*. Conversely, 21% reported feeling *somewhat unprepared,* and 16% felt *not at all prepared.*

Survey participants reported that the leading platforms for communication and instruction included email, Google, and Zoom. The majority of teachers (62%) were planning to use a blend of synchronous and asynchronous instruction, while 17% were recording all of their teaching sessions, and the 7% reported conducting only live lessons.

Just over half of the teachers surveyed indicated that students in their schools were provided with laptops or other devices (58%) and assistance with internet connectivity (53%). A surprising finding was that 63% of teachers whose schools did not plan to provide online instruction cited equity concerns as the primary reason for that decision.

Equity an Urgent Issue

Equity also emerged as the most urgent issue when participants were asked to provide an open-ended response about their top concern, with many comments specifying access to technology and family support for home learning as critical equity considerations.

Emotional Health

Additional concerns were shared regarding the emotional and physical well-being of students and teacher/educators, and the quality and rigor of online instruction, clarity of expectations for educators, support to educators for implementation of online instruction, and student engagement. Many educators also noted personal concerns, such as worries about job security and how to care for family members while teaching online.

Next Steps

As educators prepare for a new academic year, many of the largest school districts in the country have already announced that schools will not physically re-open and that learning will continue online. However, many of the areas of concern initially cited by the educators surveyed many months ago have not been sufficiently addressed. Equity considerations are even more critical now, as families with resources are hiring certified teachers to guide instruction for "pandemic pods" and micro-schools to supplement or replace the virtual instruction offered by their children's schools. Some educators who will continue teaching virtually report that they still have not had access to the training they need to feel well-prepared and to provide engaging and rigorous online instruction. Additionally, new concerns are emerging as teachers who are expected to return to a physical school express grave worries about their own health and safety. Educators also feel considerable responsibility to support their students' increased social-emotional needs and guide their classes through critical discussions regarding diversity, equity, and inclusion. Therefore, we are planning a follow-up survey to determine which areas continue to be concerns and further explore emerging issues.

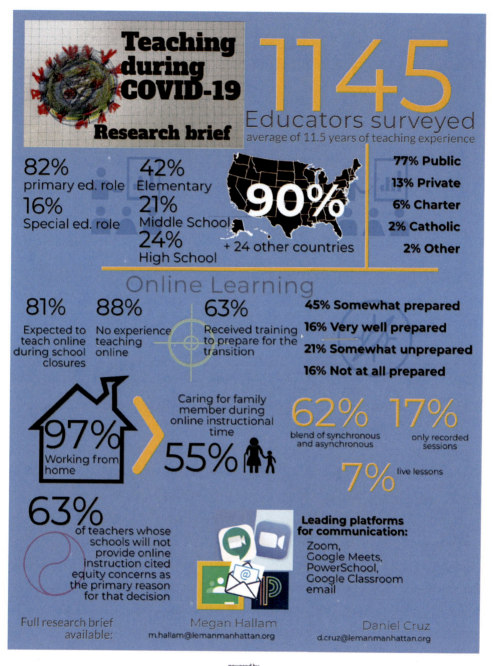

An Online Learning Expert Shares

Following is an excerpt of an eBook from Lindy Hockenbary and Educational Collaborators who kindly allowed an excerpt of the eBook to be reprinted here.

For the full experience of the book, please go to https://www.educollaborators.com/virtual/16 to download a copy of Lindy's complete eBook. It's a guide for teachers as they move instruction online and includes information on tools, techniques, and more.

Essential Components of an Online and Blended/Hybrid Course About this Chapter

Lindy Hockenbary
Instructional Technology Consultant
InTECHgrated Professional Development

http://www.intechgratedpd.org/
@lindyhockenbary

I wrote version 1 of this chapter in April of 2020 when almost every school in the entire world was forced to move to fully online learning due to COVID-19. At the time, I saw how much teachers were struggling with online learning (which makes sense being that we were never taught to teach online!). I started researching resources for online learning in K-12. Guess what? There was virtually nothing. I set out to share my knowledge of teaching online in the hopes of helping just a little. I started writing and finally had to force myself to stop.

As of the writing of this chapter, schools are sharing reopening plans for schools that include strategies such as 'live streaming' classes, which is literally the last option I would have ever come up with as a solution to provide meaningful

---

16 Educational Collaborators Virtual. Online Learning Courses/Modules. Interactive Notebooks. *Essential Components of an Online Course.* n.d. accessed July 20, 2020.

learning to all! I immediately went into the mission, "let's not make learning stink!" In response to this, I wrote an article entitled, "How do I teach students who are in physical school and remote … at the same time?[17]" at 10:00 pm one night. It exploded with over 3000 views in three days! I knew I had to get more information out there about online and blended learning and how you can teach in-person *and* remote learners.

Helping schools, teachers, and students by getting this information out as fast as possible was more important to me than perfection. I also didn't have time to get professional graphics done, so please get a good laugh at a few of my homemade graphics throughout the text!

First Things First… Online Learning Can Be Really Great!

As I write this, it is early August 2020, every school in the United States is grappling with the decision of whether to return to face-to-face school or go back to the full online learning forced upon all in the spring. I have yet to hear a single teacher, student, or parent say that they enjoyed the "virtual" or "remote" learning experience in March-June 2020; therefore, of course, no one wants to return to this remote learning scenario.

Shout this from the rooftops: *What was experienced in early 2020 was not online learning; it was crisis learning. Online learning can be really great!* For real. I completed my entire master's degree online, and I loved it.

Here is my plea to you - go into this chapter, wiping any preconceived notions of how awful online learning is from your brain. Can online learning be a bad experience? You bet. And so can face-to-face learning for many learners. I am sure everyone reading this has had a bad face-to-face learning experience. I have

---

17 Hockenbary, Lindy. Linkedin Pulse. *How do I reach students who are in physical school and remote… at the same time?* July 30, 2020. accessed August 15, 2020.

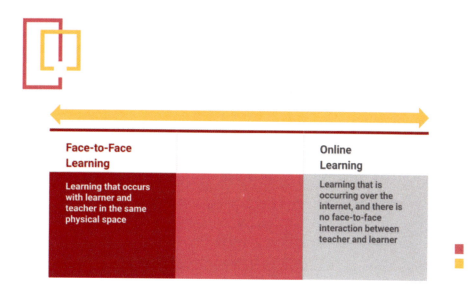

What about the middle?! That is where blended learning comes in.

Blended Learning - any combination of face-to-face learning and online learning

Any combination is a lot! What does that do to our continuum of learning models?

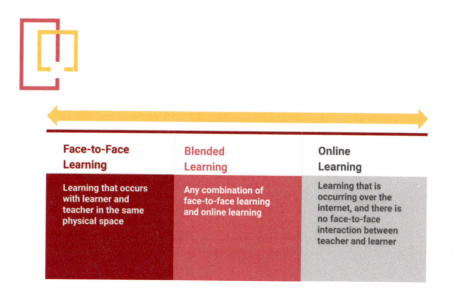

had more than one or ten bad, face-to-face learning experiences. There is good and bad online learning just as there is good and bad face-to-face learning.

To create good online learning experiences, can you recreate a typical face-to-face learning day for K-12 students? Absolutely not.

I am not saying it is easy, but it is doable. It requires an open-mind and a willingness to learn and change. You can do this.

Definitions and The Learning Model Continuum

Before we dive into the world of facilitating online and blended learning, let's make sure we are all on the same page regarding some important definitions.

Online Learning - learning that is occurring over the internet, and there is no face-to-face interaction between teacher and learner. Online learning may also be referred to as e-learning, remote learning, or distance learning.

You will hear many terms in the education field that refer to some type of online learning. Some will say these are synonyms. Some will scrutinize small differences between each term and place one term as an umbrella over another. At the end of the day, they all fall into this definition of online learning. Online learning means all content, learning tasks, communication, and collaboration are occurring virtually.

Face-to-Face Learning - learning that occurs with learner and teacher in the same physical space. Face-to-face learning may also be referred to as in-person learning or brick-and-mortar learning.

If we were to make a continuum of learning models, online learning would be on one end and face-to-face learning on the other end:

Everything in the middle of the learning model continuum is some form of blended learning.

You may have heard the term hybrid learning (especially lately). iNACOL (now the Aurora Institute) defines blended learning as follows: "**Blended learning**, also known as **hybrid learning**, is where students learn online part of the time, yet have the benefit of face-to-face instruction to maximize learning." You will see some definitions that will identify blended and hybrid learning with small differences. I lump blended and hybrid learning into the same definition. Here are two reasons why I don't separate blended and hybrid learning:

1. When you break learning models down to a continuum, these three models cover any type of learning. Blended becomes a form of hybrid, and hybrid becomes a form of blended.
2. The Aurora Institute is one of the leaders in online and blended learning research. The experts say blended and hybrid learning are the same, so I use that as my guide.

Therefore, for the purposes of this chapter, hybrid and blended learning are lumped together. For the rest of the chapter, this type of learning will be referenced as blended learning.

Almost every person in the world understands face-to-face learning because that is what we are used to. Are there many different ways to teach face-to-face? No ... not many ... millions! However, we can all picture what face-to-face learning generally looks like.

Online learning is fairly clear, although if you have never experienced a *good* online course, it may be hard to see how this is an awesome, meaningful, engaging learning option. However, contrary to the current climate, online learning really does not create device-staring zombies!

Blended learning is much more fuzzy, which makes sense since it covers a wide range of the learning model continuum. Because of this, it helps to have blended learning models. According to the Christenson Institute[18] (another leader in blended learning research), there are seven blended learning models. The best explanation of these seven models that I have found is on this site from The Christensen Institute[19] because they have great graphics that illustrate each model.

I am going to *briefly* summarize each model below, but please visit the Blended Learning Universe[20] to learn in more detail about each of the seven blended models:

- **Station Rotation**: Learners rotate through stations with at least one station focusing on an online learning component. The focus is mostly on face-to-face time.
- **Lab Rotation**: Similar to the station rotation, learners rotate through stations, but the online learning component is completed in a lab location.
- **Individual Rotation**: Learners rotate through stations but on individualized schedules, rather than in groups.
- **Flipped Classroom:** Learners gain content knowledge via online coursework and lectures (usually at home), and face-to-face time is used for teacher-guided projects. Focus is equally on the online component and face-to-face time.
- **Flex:** Learners move among learning activities according to their specific needs. Learners have a high level of control over their learning, and the focus is on the online component.
- **A La Carte:** Learners are in a traditional face-to-face learning environment but may take fully online courses in addition to their face-to-face courses. The online focus depends on how many online courses the learner is completing.
- **Enriched Virtual:** Learners complete most coursework online outside of a brick-and-mortar school building but also have supple-

---

18 Christensen Institute. n.d, accessed September 14, 2020.
19 BLU_Blended Learning Universe. Clayton Christensen Institute. n.d. accessed September 14, 2020.
20 Ibid.

mental face-to-face learning sessions with a teacher. The focus is on online learning.

Keep in mind, these models are not the be all and end all of what blended learning can look like. In fact, some learning institutions that utilize blended learning use a mix of these models (yes, a blended, blended model)!

Now that you understand the seven blended models, let's put those seven models on our learning continuum; from those that focus more on the face-to-face learning, to those that focus more on the online learning:

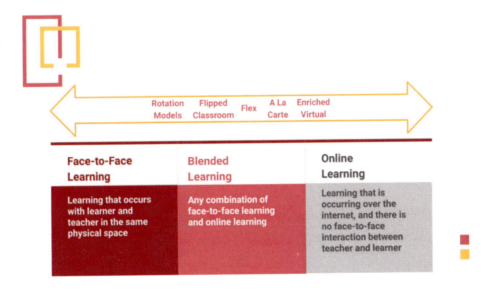

Now, there could be a lot of debate here. For example, I lumped the rotation models together, but you could argue that individual rotation is more online focused than the flipped classroom model. This is really not my point, though. My point is to show that blended models have varying focuses on face-to-face and online learning, with the rotation models having the most focus on the face-to-face learning component, and the enriched virtual model having the most focus on the online learning component.

For the rest of the chapter, instead of referring specifically to online and blended learning, I may reference the 'online component.' For online learning, this is the entire learning experience. For blended learning, this is the online part, whether or not there is a large or smaller focus for the blended course.

One more thing before we move on. I think it is helpful to consider what you can use face-to-face learning time for and online learning time for in a blended learning environment:

- Online learning time
    - Content
    - Assessments
    - Digital Collaboration
- Face-to-face learning time
    - Projects - individual or collaborative
    - Lab time
    - Discussions
    - Intervention
    - Supplementation

This is by no means a comprehensive list (not even close!). Again, what you spend time on in each format depends a lot on the blended model used, but hopefully this gives you a small peek into a blended world.

Equity

When planning and designing online and blended learning, equity should be at the forefront of all decisions. First, let's define equity. The definition of **equity,** according to Merriam-Webster, is justice according to natural law or right. But what does that mean in the context of education? Equity means making sure every student has the support they need in order to be successful. Equity in education means understanding that individual needs vary from person to person and establishing systems to ensure every learner has an equal opportunity for success.

I don't want to deep dive into the world of equity in education, as we would spend the chapter on only that topic! However, I do want to point out three factors to consider regarding equity in online and blended learning:

1. Access to technology
   - This includes access to devices and access to the internet. Has your education institution planned to ensure all learners have access?
   - Will all students be using the same device? Or will students be using devices with different operating systems (OSs)? There are so many different operating systems that some tools are compatible with and others not. If your educational institution is not providing the same device to each student, your learners may have any of the following:
     - Windows OS
     - Mac OS
     - iOS - Used on iPads and iPhones
     - Android OS - tablets or smartphones
     - Fire OS - Used on Kindles

2. Accessibility of learning materials
   - Are all learning materials provided accessible to all learners? Or do accommodations need to be made?
   - Again, I don't want to dive into accessibility, because if we did, this chapter would never end!
   - To learn more regarding how you can make your digital learning materials accessible to all, review these resources:
     - Universal Design for Learning (UDL) is a strategy designed to ensure accessibility of learning to all. UDL applies to all learning environments - online, face-to-face, blended, etc. Learn more on the UDL website[21].

---

21 CAST. *The UDL Guidelines*. n.d.. accessed September 10, 2020.

- Microsoft Educator Community course: <u>Training teachers to author accessible content</u>[22]. This course has great tips that are transferable to non-Microsoft tools.
- Microsoft Educator Community course: <u>Accessibility, Special Education, and online learning: Supporting equity in a remote learning environment</u>[23]
   ○ As you are building and curating learning materials, you can use accessibility checkers to ensure materials are accessible.
      - For Microsoft Office users: Microsoft Office documents (as well as other tools in the Microsoft suite such as <u>Sway</u>) have a built-in accessibility checker, usually found under the 'Review' tab. Learn more about the accessibility checker in the article "<u>Improve accessibility with the Accessibility Checker</u>[24],"
      - For Google Doc Suite users: <u>Grackle Docs</u> is an add-on that can be used in Google Docs, Slides, and Sheets to flag accessibility issues.
      - For websites: WebAIM has accessibility checkers for websites called <u>WAVE</u>.

3. Adult support
   ○ Is your course designed in a way that learners can complete learning tasks with minimal adult support? The answer to this will vary drastically depending on many factors, such as the age of your learners, their socioeconomic status, if your course is synchronous or asynchronous, etc.
   ○ The reason this is important to consider when designing online learning is that you, as the course designer, do not want to create a situation where success in your course is dependent on adult support; many learners may have little to no adult support at home.

---

22 Microsoft Educator Center. *Accessibility, Special Education and online learning: Supporting equity in a remote learning environment.* n.d, accessed September 12, 2020.

23 Ibid.

24 Microsoft Support. *Improve accessibility with the Accessibility Checker.* n.d. accessed September 14, 2020.

This chapter is making a large equity assumption - that all teachers and learners can access the internet in some way, shape, or form. Let's go back to our definition of online learning - learning that is occurring over the internet, and there is no face-to-face interaction between teacher and learner. Blended learning is any combination of face-to-face learning and online learning. You don't have online or blended learning without the internet! Therefore, it is hard to write about these learning environments without making this assumption of equity, which is coming from a place of extreme privilege.

The COVID-19 pandemic is shining a light on the issue of equity, and I hope it sparks change. Advocate to your education institution for equity for all.

If you are interested in learning more about equity in online learning, you can continue your learning with these resources:

- International Association of K-12 Online Learning (iNACOL) Access and Equity for All Learners in Blended and Online Education[25]
- Ten Steps to Equity in Education Policy Brief[26]

Reviewing Key Takeaways

Here are the 'key takeaways' or big ideas so far:

1. Understanding the concept that some blended learning models have more focus on online instruction is key to understanding how you could navigate the school year in any of the following scenarios:

---

25 Rose, Raymond. Rose & Smith Associates. Eric.ed.gov. iNACOL, *Access and Equity for All Learners in Blended and Online Education*. October 2014. accessed September 1, 2020.

26 OECD. Organisation for Economic Co-Operation and Development. 2008. accessed September 2, 2020.

a. If face-to-face learning is able to happen, but you have some learners who opt into full online learning.
   b. If you have a blended approach, but on staggered schedules to limit class sizes. For example, maybe learners in group A come to in-person school on Mondays and Wednesdays and engage in online learning the remainder of the week. Learners in group B would follow the same pattern but would be vice versa.
   c. Face-to-face learning happens, but the school can close at any minute.
   d. About any other scenario that is thrown at you other than 'live streaming lessons!' Don't even get me started with that (for real)!!

2. No matter the learning model followed (face-to-face, online, or blended), the pillars of teaching and learning remain the same across the learning continuum. In fact, the digital tools used remain mostly the same across the learning continuum. What changes as we move along the learning continuum is the *strategy*:

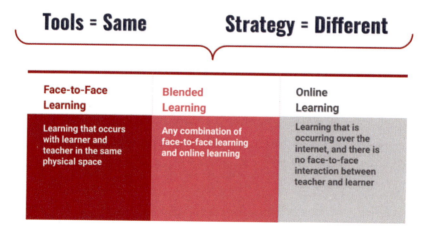

Online Learning Course Organization

There are several factors that you will want to consider regarding how you organize your course. We will go into detail on two aspects: synchronous/asynchronous and timeline.

Synchronous or Asynchronous?

The online component of learning (whether fully online or part of a blended model) can be broken down into two parts: synchronous or asynchronous? *Understanding the difference between synchronous and asynchronous learning (and what learning scenarios each is appropriate and not appropriate for) is perhaps the most important thing to understand in order to be successful designing online and blended learning experiences.*

Synchronous learning is learning that happens in *real-time*. With synchronous learning, teachers and learners are engaged in learning at the same time in the same virtual learning environment. With synchronous learning, educators set a specific time for learners to meet and conduct class. Typically, synchronous learning is facilitated through a video conferencing tool but could also be via a live chat format. The most common video conferencing tools in education are Zoom, Google Meet, and Teams meetings.

Asynchronous learning is when learners complete work related to the course on their *own schedule*. Educators provide learning materials and learning tasks that learners can review and complete at their own pace within a designated time period (for example, one week). Throughout the time period, learners may participate in discussion threads, collaborate using digital tools, or watch a video and respond to a prompt.

Asynchronous learning can have an optional synchronous component such as virtual office hours where students can seek extra help or ask questions about the week's assignments.

You could also choose a blend of synchronous and asynchronous learning. For example, the required elements of the course could be asynchronous with an optional one-hour synchronous meeting every week. There are endless options!

For full online learning, I recommend focusing on asynchronous online learning with teacher office hours offered; synchronous online learning has too many headaches for little or no benefit. However, you may be required by your education institution to facilitate synchronous learning, and that is ok! Or you may find that synchronous learning is better for your unique learners. Keep in mind; there is no wrong way to do online learning.

In fact, I highly recommend focusing on asynchronous learning, whether your learning environment is face-to-face, blended, and/or fully online.

If you would like to learn more:
- Read "Synchronous Learning vs. Asynchronous Learning in Online Education" https://thebestschools.org/magazine/synchronous-vs-asynchronous-education[27]/ to explore the pros and cons of synchronous and asynchronous learning.

COVID-19 Response: How do I teach students who are in physical school and remote ... at the same time?

Now let's talk about the COVID world scenario where you have some learners face-to-face and others that are fully online. My answer to this is focus on asynchronous learning whether your learning environment is face-to-face, blended, and/or fully online.

If you are in a personalized or individualized learning environment, this may throw a bit of a wrench into it, but never fear, it is absolutely possible and manageable! Most individualized and personalized learning environments rely

---

[27] The Best Schools. TBS Staff. *Synchronous Learning vs. Asynchronous Learning in Online Education.* September 11, 2020. accessed September 14, 2020.

on individual conferences with learner and teacher. For the online learners, simply move this part online via video conferencing tools or virtual check-ins.

If you have never taught in a personalized or individualized learning environment, you are going to need to create asynchronous content. I know that may be hard to envision, so let's look at a specific example.

Let's say we have learners in the physical school building in a face-to-face learning environment, and learners who have opted for online learning only. The learning goal is to apply the principles of design. Here is an asynchronous lesson that the teacher put together:

Intro to Design Principles https://docs.google.com/presentation/d/1voWC-Ntheoq7lKt1ElL0fr85dNYzfXBAwvKG2rezex4/edit#slide=id.g8188324404_0_518[28]

Online learners: This is an all-encompassing lesson that has everything our online learners need, and they can complete the lesson at any time, at their *own pace*.

Face-to-face learners: Why can't our face-to-face learners do the exact same lesson at their *own pace*, but the time is set to the face-to-face learning time?

This example allows students to work at their own pace whether in a brick-and-mortar school building or at home. It doesn't matter if some students are at home and others are in physical school. Both are focused on the online component - one synchronously and one asynchronously.

If I am a teacher, I can assign this asynchronous lesson and use my face-to-face class time to check in with my remote learners, answer questions, walk around the room and check-in with in-person learners, provide real-time feedback, etc. My time is opened up to spend time supporting both face-to-face and online

---

28 Hockenbary, Lindy. *Asynchronous Lesson – Intro to Design Principles*. n.d. accessed September 14, 2020.

learners because my lesson is digital. Technology allows me to basically duplicate myself in video form to all of my learners regardless of *when* they are learning.

In the above scenario, the students in physical school are experiencing a blended model, and the remote students are experiencing full online learning. The exact blended model used could vary but is most likely some form of the Enriched Virtual or Flex models. The Enriched Virtual model keeps the focus on the online learning and face-to-face learning time is viewed as *supplemental*. That sounds like a great 'pandemic' learning model to me. The remote students are working mostly asynchronously, but this doesn't mean there can't be a synchronous component.

Maybe you have a 'class meeting' every morning, and it is optional for the full online learners to join. Use this time to focus on the social-emotional side of learning, develop relationships with your learners, and build a strong learning culture.

But how do we take attendance if our online learners are working mostly asynchronously, and the synchronous component is optional? *Attendance should never be measured by being synchronously in a virtual space.* Instead, don't take attendance and focus on competency-based learning.

In this example, I would assess whether my online learners met the learning goal of applying the design principles. What else should matter? My synchronous time is spent on social-emotional goals, so it is not mandatory. However, I could record for my online learners to watch later if they wish.

In summary, if you focus on asynchronous online learning, you can make learning work for on-site and off-site learners. You get a ton of 'bang for your buck' with asynchronous online learning.

Personal Connections

Creating and maintaining personal connections with students is a critical part of the teaching and learning process, because the student-teacher relationship forms the foundation for all learning. For a full online environment, you may be thinking, "How do I develop a learning relationship with a student that I never see in person?!" It is true that cultivating relationships looks *different* in an online setting than a face-to-face setting, but the importance is no less or less possible. There are many ways you can develop relationships with your students in an online learning environment. We will share four specific strategies to get you started, but keep in mind, these strategies are in no way meant to be a comprehensive list of strategies for cultivating connections with students in online learning. I will focus mostly on online learning in this section because these strategies are essential to a fully online course and more optional for blended learning since you do have some face-to-face time.

1:1 Appointments

Open up your calendar periodically for fifteen-minute one-on-one appointments with learners where you can join a video call or phone call together. Most calendar tools have an appointment feature that will allow you to set up a block of appointments on your calendar that other people can reserve.

Google Calendar users: How to set up appointment slots in Google Calendar. https://support.google.com/calendar/answer/190998?co=GENIE.Platform%3D-Desktop&hl=en[29]

Outlook users: There are several add-ins for Outlook:
- Microsoft Bookings
- Calendly
- FindTime
- Scheduler

Educator Kristin Wolfgang uses SignUpGenius for parent/guardian meetings.

---

29 Google Support. *Use Google Calendar appointment slots*. n.d. accessed September 14, 2020.

You may even make 1:1 appointments with learners a requirement of your online or blended course to ensure you are connecting with each and every student.

More Resources for Online and Blended/Hybrid Learning

- Ditch that Textbook has a large list of e-learning resources[30]
- If needed, you could provide planner templates or guides to your learners. Examples:
  - Daily schedule planner
  - Daily Agenda
- Educator Remote Learning Groups:
  - Facebook Educator Temporary School Closure for Online Learning
    - This group was so popular they have created sub-groups for different content areas, grade levels, specialists, etc. Links to join the specialty groups are in this doc.[31]

G Suite for Edu (Google) Districts

- Google Teacher Center distance learning resources[32]
- This slide deck is a great intro to what you can do in G Suite for remote learning.[33]

---

30 Ditch That Texbook. *An Educator's Resource for Distance Learning, Remote Learning, and eLearning.* n.d. accessed September 14, 2020.

31 Global Educator Support Group Directory. Global Educator Collective. n.d. accessed September 14, 2020.

32 Google for Education. Teacher Cente., *Enabling Distance Learning.* n.d. accessed September 14, 2020.

33 Google for Education. *Distance Learning Strategies with G Suite and Chromebooks.* n.d. accessed September 14, 2020.

Microsoft 365 for Edu Districts

Microsoft Teams for Education
- Remote Learning Team - Complete this form to join[34]
- Getting Started:
  - Get started with Microsoft Teams for remote learning[35]
- Educator/Student:
  - Remote teaching and learning with Office 365[36]
  - Schedule a Parent-Teacher of Staff Conference Using Office 365[37]
  - Use Microsoft Translator to Host a Multilingual Parent-Teacher Conference[38]
  - Engage Students in Distance Learning with Apps and Content from Microsoft's Partners[39]
- Training/Tips:
  - Teams EDU Webinars[40]

---

34 Microsoft Enable Remote Learning Community form to join. n.d. accessed September 14, 2020.

35 Microsoft Docs. Microsoft 365. *Getting started with Microsoft Teams for remote learning.* August 19, 2020. accessed September 14, 2020.

36 Microsoft Support. *Remote reaching and learning in Office 365 Education.* Microsoft Teams for Education. n.d. accessed September 14, 2020.

37 Microsoft Support. *Schedule a parent-teacher or staff conference using Office 365.* n.d. accessed September 14, 2020.

38 Microsoft Support. *Use Microsoft Translator to host a multilingual parent-teacher conference.* n.d. accessed September 14, 2020.

39 Microsoft Educator Center. *Engage Students in Remote Learning with Apps and Content from Microsoft Partners.* n.d. accessed September 14, 2020.

40 Microsoft. *Microsoft Teams for Education Webinar Series.* n.d. accessed September 14, 2020.

- - MEC: Getting Started with Online Learning in Office 365[41]
- Microsoft Teams for EDU Scenarios:
  - K12[42]
  - MEC: Professional Development OneStop[43]

Parting Thoughts From Lindy

Don't try to create an online or blended course overnight. Slowly build the course piece by piece. See what works/what doesn't work and make small edits along the way.

Educators are very creative, and you will find a way to teach things that you never would have thought could be taught in an online setting. Public speaking has been taught as an online college class since about 2000 (yes, that's 20 years)! I saw a video on Twitter of students practicing swimming techniques without a pool!

Remember, online learning can be fantastic! Most of all, enjoy the process. Don't forget to have fun and focus on maintaining/developing relationships with your learners.

Another Online Learning Expert Weighs In

How can teachers engage with students online? - Adrian Segar

Whenever teachers speak to all students, in person or online, they are the sole source of engagement in the classroom. Let's call this *broadcast-style* engagement. Almost every student will be passively listening to the teacher. The other form

---

41 Microsoft Educator Center. *Getting started with hybrid learning in Office 365.* n.d. accessed September 14, 2020.

42 Flipgrid. Teams K12. *How do you use Microsoft Teams?* November 4, 2019. accessed September 14, 2020.

43 Microsoft. Educator Center. *Microsoft's education professional development and training resources. Start here!* n.d. accessed September 14, 2020.

of classroom engagement is one that occurs through participation in an activity with other students, which I'll call *active* engagement.

To optimize classroom learning, we need to keep in mind the words of Ivan Illich: "Most learning is not the result of instruction. It is rather the result of unhampered participation in a meaningful session."[44] Active engagement involves significantly more participation than broadcast-style engagement.

These considerations lead to modern in-person classroom formats, where teachers provide core content and insights to students in short broadcast-style oral or written segments, and then transition to individual and/or small-group opportunities for students to digest, reflect on, and respond to what they have heard or read. The class reconvenes to share group learning and insights. The teacher then supplies more introductory material and introduces a new small-group activity, and the learning cycle repeats.

Because it's harder for a teacher to possess the same level of student awareness and supervision possible in an in-person classroom, online learning environments need to shift control of learning from teacher to student to some degree. Maintaining active engagement *between* students online becomes a crucial component for successful online learning.

Unfortunately, when transitioning from in-person to online classrooms, teachers initially often reduce or eliminate time for active engagement. Typically, students are switched between broadcast lesson units and working alone. Individual work is not supervised while it's taking place, and small group work disappears.

Luckily, many online learning platforms include facilities for supporting individual and small group work, allowing students to work alone or with each other. Teachers can move around and supervise and support, just as they would do in a physical classroom.

---

44 *Deschooling Society*, Harper & Row, 1971

I'll illustrate using the popular Zoom meeting platform, but teachers can facilitate and support active engagement on any platform that allows students to be moved in and out of small individual workgroups.

Zoom's *breakout rooms* functionality makes it easy to create small on-the-fly workgroups for student topic or issue exploration, discussion, and reports. Zoom can create these groups *automatically*, assigning students randomly into evenly sized rooms. In my experience, rooms with three or four students per group work best. Or, if a teacher prefers to choose the members in each group, Zoom allows the teacher to manually populate each small group from the list of students present.

Before students are moved into their small groups, the teacher explains what each group is to do, and the time allotted for the task. Once the groups have begun, the teacher can join any group to check on progress and provide support. When the allotted time is up, the teacher can close all groups (with a pre-close warning message, if desired) and bring all students back to the main meeting.

Finally, it's worth pointing out that if teachers want to supervise students working independently, they can simply move every student into their own breakout room. (Zoom can supply up to 50, which should be ample for most classrooms.) The teacher, as Zoom host, can easily visit individual breakout rooms to check in with any student.

By using online platforms that support both whole class broadcast *and* small group work, teachers can create and foster the active engagement in their classrooms necessary to optimize classroom learning.

Adrian Segar is an educator, facilitator, and meeting designer who works globally to facilitate connection, learning, and engagement, wherever and however people meet. He is the author of three books on meeting design, including *The Power of Participation*: a tool chest of simple meeting processes that significantly improve all kinds of classes, sessions, and gatherings. Learn more about Adrian Segar at https://www.conferencesthatwork.com, which includes over five hundred articles on ways to make learning better for teachers, presenters, and students.

Summary and Recommendations

Triage or emergency teaching happened in classrooms worldwide from March 2020 to the end of the school year when schools closed to the COVID-19 pandemic. Teachers stepped up and did the best they could to keep students on track, to use new tools for instruction, and to support online learning.

Online learning didn't stop at the end of the 2019-2020 school year. The COVID-19 pandemic changed life as we knew it for the immediate future.

Administrators wanting success in the classroom should invest in professional development using teachers like Lindy Hockenbary to retool their teachers, and experts like Adrian Segar to provide insight on how new tools can transform teaching.

> ▶ **School Leadership Committee Takeaway**
>   - What happened from March to the end of the school year was online emergency teaching.
>   - Have teachers now embraced instruction through online learning – or has their willingness to move forward been damaged by the experience of being thrown into an instructional method they had not previously used?
>   - How will you bring teachers into new professional development for online learning, showing the possibilities while acknowledging the hasty nature at the end of the school year?
>   - Reviewing the graphic and description of the survey of nearly 1200 teachers conducted by Daniel Cruze and Megan Storey Hallam described in this chapter, how might your teachers compare in experience before the school closed for COVID?

- Had your teachers been exposed to online learning previously?
- Were there online learning courses in place at your school?
- Was there online learning professional development before the school closing?
○ What are your plans for teacher professional development to teach online learning tools?
○ What are your plans for teacher professional development to teach pedagogy for online learning?
○ Will you implement:
  - Synchronous learning?
    - Note that the educators interviewed and much research indicate synchronous learning for many hours daily in front of a screen is physically and mentally taxing for participants.
  - Asynchronous learning?
  - Hybrid/blended learning?
○ How did emergency remote learning/triage learning unfold at your school?
  - Did you reinforce existing learning, or were teachers able to introduce new concepts?
    - How would teachers rate their ability to adapt to online learning quickly?

Chapter 8 – Cybersecurity and Technology

Introduction

A key concern shared by educators interviewed was: What happens when school devices suddenly go to students' homes? The technology educators were used to keeping networks and devices secure at their schools or districts. Significant resources had been invested to maintain safety, security, and privacy. Software was carefully vetted according to federal law and practices.

Many districts and schools already had emergency plans to continue education in case of a crisis, but the crises envisioned were two weeks or less in duration. This pandemic caused nearly all schools to be closed from March to the end of the school year.

Online learning suddenly became the prevalent instructional method. For those schools already equipped for 1-to-1 that had already sent devices home to students, security had been addressed.

However, most schools were not fully prepared for 1-to-1 devices to go home throughout K-12.

This chapter needed experts equipped with the know-how, existing research, expertise, and connection to schools to write this chapter. Susan Davis and Christina Lewellen of ATLIS filled the bill on all counts. They kindly agreed to put together a primer on what schools and districts need to know and address for security, privacy, and best practices.

Cybersecurity and the School Technology Department

Susan Davis, Professional Development Director, ATLIS
Christina Lewellen, Executive Director, ATLIS

We would like to extend a special thanks to our public-school colleagues who have helped in the preparation of this chapter:

Monty Hitschler, Director of I.S. & Technologies, Government and Educational Services, Rockport MA

Bobby Bardenhagen, Director of Technology, Orinda Union School District, Orinda CA

Who Addresses Security at Schools

Who is responsible for securing school networks and data?

Even under normal circumstances, this question proves challenging for many in education. Technology personnel, of course, can do their part by patching software, managing firewalls, and encrypting devices, but the fact is that the growing sophistication of phishing and ransomware attacks manipulate the human vulnerabilities of end users, not necessarily the devices and systems they use, through sophisticated social engineering techniques. Likewise, the human factor comes into play with anyone who has access to the data collected and used by a school or district -- and who may not handle it as carefully as it warrants. How can school technology personnel protect against someone who opens a seemingly innocuous attachment and unleashes a slew of hidden files that can hold a network hostage? How can the tech team protect school data when critical office personnel download data onto their hard drives for easier access at home and essentially risk putting that data into the hands of… well, anyone?

Cybersecurity efforts, even in the best of times, require an all-school, full-on team effort. As schools sent their students, faculty, and other personnel to work and learn from home during the COVID-19 pandemic, the matter of protecting the school's resources and users' personal data was compounded. Add to this the rapid increase in cyber-attacks during a time of crisis, many of which targeted home networks, and the need for sound cybersecurity practices, including awareness, policies, and procedures, becomes paramount. The need for vigilant and consistent measures to make school digital spaces safe amounts to what the National Association of Independent Schools (NAIS) has termed a "standard of care" that schools are obliged to address.

The recommendations in this chapter evolve from the ATLIS Cybersecurity Recommendations and ATLIS360, a self-audit program for schools, along with many workshops and presentations created to support those recommendations, and research conducted during the COVID-19 pandemic. Throughout this chapter, we refer to schools in general, whether they are private or public institutions, as we understand their overlapping cyber safety concerns. When we say school, we mean school or district, unless a specific type of school or district is specifically named.

Leading Cybersecurity Efforts
Building and Sustaining an All-School/All-District Team Effort

Establishing a team of key school constituents to focus on cybersecurity issues is essential. Such a team provides a means for continuous improvement and self-education to address what is, by definition, a rapidly moving target. The team, generally speaking, should adopt the following ongoing tasks:

- Assessing the school's current cybersecurity plans, resources, and measures;

- Assessing and updating the knowledge level of the team members;
- Conducting an annual review of the school's cybersecurity stance, policies and procedures, the threat landscape, training programs, and insurance coverage;
- Periodically, but at minimum every three years, overseeing and responding to an external audit of the school's cybersecurity.

During a time of crisis, such a team provides a much-needed command central for a school's cybersecurity efforts.

Team members become a school's clearinghouse for staying informed and sharing information. The team supports and promotes a culture of cyber safety through communication and training. Team members provide a home base for developing and implementing school continuity plans. In particular, the team should be responsible for designing a bank of Digital Security Policies and Procedures (as recommended in *ATLIS360*), which encompasses several specific plans (detailed below); the team should also take responsibility for sustaining the policies and procedures required to those plans. Such plans include:

- Emergency Response Plan
- IT Disaster Recovery Plan
- Pandemic Preparedness Plan
- Business Continuity Plan
- Cyber Incident Response Plan
- Crisis Communication Plan
- Network and Software Applications Permissions Policy
- End-User Security Agreement

Policies and Procedures
The Data Landscape

The cybersecurity and safety team not only keeps its pulse on the actions of bad actors but should also seek a clear perspective of the school or district's data landscape. Who are its critical users? Where is it most vulnerable? If these individuals are not on the team, how are they kept up-to-date and informed? A clear understanding of how data is managed at the school allows personnel to make strategic decisions needed for cyber safety. Establishing and maintaining that understanding is enhanced when time is given to creating a detailed map of the school's data that includes how data is entered, transferred, and used (and by whom) within any school system. Such a Map of Data Flow Through the Schools Information Systems, recommended in the *ATLIS360 Self-Audit Guide for Technology in Schools,* should:

- Allow for targeted training for managing users and for training and implementing procedures;
- Provide a basis for deeper conversations and understanding about data protection issues.

Multi-Factor Authentication

Implementing multi-factor authentication (MFA) for all who handle sensitive data at the school is a vital first step. Such a procedure should include anyone who interacts with student and employee records. At a minimum, this should include administrators, teachers, and other personnel who interact with data. Even the cleaning crew with only email access should have MFA. An identity provider or SSO manager like One Login can make this process easier to manage.

Multi-factor authentication is generally accepted as the best way to get the "most bang for your buck" as far as securing school resources and data are concerned.

Training and Communication

Requiring frequent, up-to-date, and ongoing training for all users of school devices and cloud services is essential. Phishing simulators can serve as a great tool for targeting the most vulnerable employee populations for training, saving the technology team precious time. Targeted phishing training should include anyone who uses the school's email system, which is the top source of cyber penetration attacks (*ATLIS Cybersecurity Threat Assessment*). This group can include parents and volunteers, as well as Board members, depending on who has a school email account.

An uptick in cyber-attacks and phishing incidents during the COVID-19 pandemic meant that such training was even more critical. The need for frequent communications and reminders about cyber safety became apparent as more users worked from home and were targeted by bad actors (those who would wreak havoc online.)

As new employees are onboarded or trained in new technologies, it is important to embed an understanding of personally identifiable information (PII) and cybersecurity with their training from the beginning. This embedded understanding relates to training for specific tools such as the Student Information System, accounting systems, etc.

All users should be instructed about and required to use safe password practices.

IT Responsibilities

There are many areas where the IT team can make a difference in the cybersecurity of the schools they serve. These steps are critical to the safety and security of schools and should not be overlooked. The IT team should:

- Provide for secure and adequate back-ups for all necessary school data, whether on-premises, in the cloud, or off-site. It should help develop and test a disaster recovery plan;
- Be alert to the details of Cloud systems. The IT team should carefully review its service agreements for handling data, disaster recovery, etc. It should not make the mistake of assuming, as sometimes happens, that all systems are necessarily safe in a Cloud environment;
- Assure that anti-virus and malware protection is up-to-date and patched on all school devices;

- Implement total drive encryption first for all employees who have access to or use privileged data (admission, advancement, business, medical, etc.), then for all school-owned devices;
- Monitor and maintain adequate firewall protection for the school network. It should employ regular network security scans;
- Review security settings on all school-owned devices to determine appropriate levels;
- Segment critical servers and services from the broader school network.

School Personnel Responsibilities

Because so many cybersecurity concerns reside in the individual employee's practices, it is important to create a culture in which each stakeholder assumes individual responsibility for cyber safety and security. All personnel should:

- Become informed about and stay current on cyber threats, including the changing landscape of phishing and other attacks through email;
- Welcome ongoing cybersecurity training as a professional responsibility;
- Be attentive to best practices for handling privileged data;
- Use passwords and password vaults responsibly.

Privacy Statements

During the recent pandemic, many vendors made a myriad of useful (and questionably useful) tools available to the education community. As educators attempted to solve the problems of delivering content in an online environment, many eagerly embraced these tools without consulting their technology colleagues. Some schools with established vetting processes experienced teachers "going rogue" to select the tools they felt they needed, whether this was using a preferred video conferencing application or even employing a substitute Learning Management System (LMS).

Not only did this create unnecessary complication and duplication of tools and processes for students and their families, but unfortunately, not all tools are created equal when it comes to privacy issues. A school or district's edtech leadership or cyber safety team should be trained to review the policies of digital tools and work with teachers to select those that are right for their circumstances. If a tool's privacy statements do not adequately address school compliance requirements such as FERPA, HIPPA, and GDPR, it should be rejected.

Thus, it is important that schools implement and enforce a review process for vetting new applications and software. Users should be required to submit new applications and tools for review with regard to data safety and security for school users. At the same time, the process should encourage exploration and innovation by faculty—a tricky dance for school technology leaders to execute. This give and take should be reflected in a clearly stated and practically enforceable Network and Software Applications Permissions Policy and End-User Security Agreement, as recommended in *ATLIS360*.

This problem of vetting tools is an ongoing issue for schools as innovations for edtech arrive on the scene on an almost daily basis. In the end, the education of users about the "why" for such a process may be key to gaining the buy-in for such a process to work properly.

When Devices Go Home

If good cybersecurity measures are already in place in the school setting, then the focus during a school emergency can be on the special circumstances this new arrangement requires. During a situation like the COVID-19 pandemic and the resulting transition to virtual schooling, the following considerations come into play:

- Tech teams should review admin privileges on school-owned laptops before sending them out into the wild. Settings may need to be opened up to allow students and teachers to connect to networks,

etc., in their home environment. Similarly, new safety settings may need to be implemented for devices sent home for use by students;
- Some attention should be given to determining home network vulnerabilities. For those who handle sensitive data, it may be necessary to implement a Virtual Private Network (VPN) for the greatest protection outside the school network; (See resources from the SANS Institute.)
- The cyber safety and security team should develop and communicate remote working policies and procedures, including mobile secure device policies;
- The technology team should conduct network scans and secure backups with vigilance;
- The cyber safety and security team should continue regular training and mock phishing campaigns, reinforce needs for MFA and VPN use, insist on password complexity, and stress the importance of using devices only for work and not sharing with family;
- Edtech coaches should provide guidance for video conferencing and collaboration tools, in particular with regard to safe security settings. Many of the problems from video conference "bombing," for example, that evolved over the course of the spring of 2020, were directly related to the unchanged, less-than-secure default settings of the tools used. This "bombing" involved outside people gaining access to video sessions and introducing profanity and inappropriate images;
- The cyber safety and security team should communicate ongoing, updated information about developments in cybersecurity. For example, during the COVID-19 disruption, cyberattacks were reported to have increased "fivefold" (World Health Organization).

Cybersecurity remains a critical focal point for schools as they attempt to maintain a standard of care for cyber safety for their constituents. Yet the heavy lift of transitioning to a new digital learning environment and providing the support needed to keep schools running during the pandemic of 2020 tested the limits of the personnel who would typically serve as the cyber safety watchkeepers in schools. At the same time, the strain of at least a fivefold increase in cyberattacks meant that the need for implementing and sustaining good cybersecurity measures tested the personnel tasked with keeping schools safe to the utmost. The move to at-home work and school further emphasized the need for every individual associated with a school to have up-to-date cybersecurity training and awareness. Now that schools that dealt with this crisis and tested the limits of their continuity plans have had time to reflect, they have been given a rare chance to reflect on how well their staffing and policies held up and to establish practical and efficient programs and protocols to keep schools cyber safe into the future.

Summary

Schools reflecting on the months of emergency online learning will benefit from conducting the audits and renewing their policies and procedures recommended by Ms. Davis and Ms. Lewellen. These threats intensified during the pandemic but will not lessen anytime in the future.

Resources

Association of Technology Leaders in Independent Schools. ATLIS Cyber Threat Assessment. PDF. 2018. (Available to ATLIS Members via Document Library.)

Association of Technology Leaders in Independent Schools. ATLIS Cybersecurity Recommendations. Revised 2018.

Association of Technology Leaders in Independent Schools. ATLIS360: A Technology Self-Study Guide for Schools. PDF. 2020.

Katie Fritchen, The State of K-12 Cyber Safety and Security: Remote Learning Cybersecurity Lessons for the New School Year, Security Boulevard, 2 July 2020.

Robert Olsen and Matt Flora, Coronavirus (COVID-19) Cybersecurity and Continuity Considerations, Ankura presentation at ATLIS Annual Conference, 6 April 2020.

SANS Institute. <u>Creating a Cyber Secure Home.</u> Downloadable poster.

Sunil Sharma, <u>Remote Learning: Tips for Schools and Educational Institutions to Secure Themselves from Cyber Threats</u>, *Express Learning*, 15 July 2020.

Wendy Silverman, <u>Cybersecurity in Independent Schools: Data Breach Threats and Prevention Techniques</u>, National Association of Independent Schools Legal Brief, December 2018.

Kim Thomas. <u>Building a Secure Home Network.</u> SANS Institute, 2020. PDF.

World Health Organization, <u>WHO Reports Fivefold Increase in Cyber Attacks, Urges Vigilance</u>, 23 April 2020.

- **School Leadership Committee Takeaway**
  - You will want your technology director/CIO/CTO on your committee not just for this chapter but as a standing committee member.
  - When was the latest technology audit done at your school?
    - How was cybersecurity addressed in that audit?
    - How was privacy addressed in that audit?
  - Was your family data accurate in March when schools closed?
    - If not, what is your plan to keep data accurate so that family data is always up-to-date?
  - Do you have 1-to-1 for all children in your school?
    - If so, do they take the devices home?
    - If not, what is the plan to move forward with 1-to-1? Computing devices are the textbooks of today—necessary for learning.
    - How are you addressing providing devices and Internet for families that cannot afford these?
    - If you used CARES or other money to purchase devices, how will you replace those devices in 3-5 years?

- What security issues arose during the closing of schools when devices went home, sometimes for the first time?
  - How did you solve these issues?
  - Were you able to have parents sign for devices or, like many schools, did you skip that step so that every child had a device?
    - What are the pros and cons of skipping signatures for devices?
- Reviewing the plans listed in this chapter (listed below), which do you have in place? What do you need to address?
  - Emergency Response Plan
  - IT Disaster Recovery Plan
  - Pandemic Preparedness Plan
  - Business Continuity Plan
  - Cyber Incident Response Plan
  - Crisis Communication Plan
  - Network and Software Applications Permissions Policy
  - End-User Security Agreement

Chapter 9 – Summary and Recommendations

An Extraordinary Time

We lived through an extraordinary time. Everything turned upside down when COVID-19 struck the world. Entire countries were ordered to stay home to stop the virus from spreading. Schools closed, learning shifted to remote instruction, people got sick and sometimes died, many lost their jobs, some hoarded sanitizer and toilet paper. It all happened so quickly. Sometimes it's hard to remember a time when we stood close to one another, shook hands, went to movies, played basketball, worked out at gyms, attended concerts, and regularly flew on airplanes.

- Most of these things will return. Perhaps by the time you read this, a new normal will have emerged.
- For schools, COVID-19 was a lesson in triage. These things happened chronologically or simultaneously:
- School staff reached out to families to ensure kids were safe
- Administrators arranged food distribution for children
- Curriculum and technology experts created and delivered professional development for teachers
- School staff reached out to students and families to share the instructional plan and to check on how they were managing
- Technology staff provided computing devices and the Internet for kids without access
- Teachers tried to reinforce existing knowledge while checking the social-emotional health of kids

Notice that "introduce new concepts" wasn't on the list. That's because the schools interviewed made a decision not to take this time to implement true online learning with a new curriculum. Mostly schools managed to deliver remote emergency learning, sometimes through technology, sometimes through packets of handouts.

Students Fell Through the Cracks

Some students were missed or underserved. Often there weren't devices or the Internet to provide students without them and no money to purchase new devices. Interviewees for this book found creative ways to get computers to kids or to create low tech workarounds.

Some schools tapped their budgets to provide computers. New York City distributed devices and the Internet to every child without a computer; Philadelphia did as well. Other schools and districts made 1-to-1 a reality for students for the first time.

Special education students couldn't get the kind of attention they needed and deserved. Teachers tried to reach students through online learning, but often that was ineffective.

ESL or ELL students couldn't continue language learning guided by in-person teachers.

Remote Emergency Learning, Triage Learning

Educators interviewed frequently mentioned the emergency nature of online learning. COVID-19 learning was not the ideal, well-thought-out instruction schools want for children. Teachers stepped up to learn new tools and reach students.

While immersed in online learning, teachers were mostly not exposed to meaningful online learning techniques. In the future, school leaders will want to provide thorough and ongoing professional development to all teachers, even if they have returned to face-to-face instruction.

It's been a time of experimentation and reflection, of mandating technology tools, of reaching out to families, of helping teachers use tools they'd never used and try instructing in ways they'd never known.

Schools have been through an extraordinary time. School leaders will want to spend time on a post-mortem of how they fared at the end of 2020. See the proposed questions at the end of this chapter for a starting document.

Let's review the journey through the learnings from educators and examine what can happen next.

The Learnings and Recommendations

Thirty-two wise educators shared what got them through the COVID-19 crisis and what they recommended for the future.

Digital Equity/Food Insecurity

Many children rely on food from their school district, up to 30 million in the U.S. as of 2016. Struggling families know that, even if they cannot always provide, their children enrolled in schools will get meals. School meals stopped when schools closed. The same will happen for any future emergency. Public schools will want to continually check their ability to prepare and deliver food.

https://www.washingtonpost.com/education/a-national-crisis-as-coronavirus-forces-many-schools-online-this-fall-millions-of-disconnected-students-are-being-left-behind/2020/08/16/458b04e6-d7f8-11ea-9c3b-dfc394c03988_story.html[45]

---

45 Balingit, Moriah. The Washington Post. Education. *'A national crisis': As coronavirus forces many schools online this fall, millions of disconnected students are being left behind.* August 16, 2020. accessed September 1, 2020.

Recommendation: The homework gap is real. Children need devices and access to the Internet for learning. Technology has moved from being an option to a necessity. It's time to revamp the budget and find ways to support children with 1-to-1 at home.

Social-Emotional Health and Learning (Chapter 3)

Mr. Ethan Delavan provided a thorough look at the benefits and types of social-emotional learning/health programs that schools can utilize. The major recommendation from this chapter is that all schools should consider a program and implement it not just during crises but always. The stronger a school community is, the better they are able to weather the ups and downs of daily life as well as unusual times.

Recommendations

- Social-emotional health training for all teachers, staff, counselors, and administrators is recommended
    - See Chapter 3 to learn about the different research-based social-emotional health and learning programs that exist. School staff will want to determine which program best fits their culture, demographics, and educational philosophy
- Initial social-emotional health surveys of all teachers, students, staff, and parents will provide a baseline
- Social-emotional health surveys at regular interviews, with more intense surveying for crises, is recommended

Leadership (Chapter 4)

Leadership is a quality that has many definitions, yet during a crisis, effective leadership is recognizable and makes a difference to the outcome. The same leaders who sensibly and authentically guide schools through a crisis also steer schools through less chaotic times.

Recommendations

- Leaders during a crisis will want to step in, gauge the school climate and social-emotional health, and take action
- Looking to core values, as Dr. McLeod has described, will help ground leaders' responses
- Leaders with solid relationships with other leaders, staff, parents, and students will perform well
- Acknowledging the crisis or other events allows community members and stakeholders to feel heard and validated
- Communicating frequently, through multiple venues, ensures that everyone sees and understands the message
- Encouraging feedback and a willingness to listen helps stakeholders with their concerns and questions
- As Dr. McLeod explains, there are different phases during an emergency. Leaders will want to understand the various phases and move towards deeper learning and innovation as soon as this makes sense
- Authenticity in word and action will ground leaders and gain respect from the school community. Honesty, while leading, will move a school towards a positive outcome.

Relationships (Chapter 5)

Teachers work hard to build relationships with their students and with parents. Relationships will always be needed even when instruction is delivered differently.

Recommendations

School districts should ensure that their professional development for teachers is not just about learning tools and techniques for teaching online. Exploring ways to engage with, establish, and nurture relationships with students is essential.

Communication (Chapter 6)

In a crisis, sometimes there is a tendency to hold back communication, waiting until everything solidifies. However, school districts that communicated early, frequently, and thoughtfully helped their districts most successfully weather the storm of COVID-19. Chapter author Mike Daugherty provided exemplars of how and when to communicate. Communication was the thread holding communities together through unheard of times.

Recommendations

- Survey your school community about communication and other factors from COVID-19
- Revamp the communication plan to make sure you are addressing avenues and frequency of communication, both during day-to-day and emergencies

Online Learning/Teachers/Schedule (Chapter 7)

Lindy Hockenbary stepped us through online learning. She described the difference between synchronous and asynchronous learning and explained hybrid or blended learning.

Recommendations

Professional Development is not a "one and done", especially when the entire mode of instruction has shifted. Continuing Professional Development, support networks for teachers, outside and inside presenters, and a way to help teachers track their progress is recommended.

Cybersecurity and the Technology Department, and Infrastructure (Chapter 8)

Many security issues are introduced when devices go into student homes and use family networks. Privacy, safety, and best practices need revisiting. Susan

Davis and Christina Lewellen outlined the plans that technology departments will want to create.

Recommendations

School leaders will want to explore the links that ATLIS provides. Even though ATLIS was created for independent school technology leaders, they are collaborative with public and charter schools. Their workshops are affordable and useful.

Parents

Parents struggled during COVID-19. Many parents lost their jobs. Some parents were required to go to work in possibly unsafe conditions. Parents suddenly had children at home when they were usually working during the school day. Parents who were teachers had to care for their children and provide homeschooling support as their children learned while teaching their students.

Recommendations

Treat parents with grace and compassion. Survey parents frequently to assess their and their children's social-emotional health and offer support, kindness, and flexibility.

Students

Life was tough for students during COVID-19. Some acted out. Some students "ghosted" and disappeared. Some students fell through the cracks and didn't get food, devices, the Internet, and the type of teaching they needed. Some experienced anxiety, stress, and depression. Most students missed their friends, their teachers, and school in general.

But reports indicated many students were resilient. Students, unlike adults, are in the tumult of growth and change continually. Their bodies are growing and changing; what they know and understand is increasing daily. Their ideas and beliefs are being formed. Many of the educators interviewed said that, overall, students will be okay.

Christine Triano, a psychologist in Los Angeles, wrote in *Psychology Today*: *"As for our teens, they too had to sit with disappointment. But then, they were largely fine. … Yes, they missed seeing friends in person as much as they would like. They may have even pushed to get out more than felt safe or possible. But the teen brain is nothing if not wired to seek connection with peers, and thanks to the range of virtual options available, for the most part they kept the channels open."* Quoted with permission from *https://www.psychologytoday.com/us/blog/the-adolescent-mind/202008/back-school-back-stress* [46]

Recommendations

Teachers will likely ask students to reflect on this unusual time. Teachers and counselors should check in on students, and school leaders should conduct surveys or check-ins. School leaders will want to plan a comprehensive online learning plan that includes social-emotional health for students and teachers.

Opportunities

We can choose how to face the future. Lying beneath the uncertainty is the opportunity to recalibrate. We've been trying to make school learner-centered for some time. Online learning, by its very nature, puts learners in the driving seat. Teachers realized soon into the COVID-19 pandemic that the whole classroom experience doesn't translate when your students are in front of screens.

Recalibration can be about challenging our assumptions about school. It can involve reexamining budgets, schedules, professional development, and programs.

---

46 Triano, Christine. Psychology Today. *Back to School, Back to Stress, Checking in at the end of the pandemic summer.* August 30, 2020. accessed September 3, 2020

Schools can have a much-needed reset if this opportunity is seized.

Major Conclusion: We Can't Go Back

Even though we've been exposed to an imperfect and rushed version of online learning, the schools interviewed agreed that we can't go fully back to only the old ways of learning. It's now time to make this new dynamic work effectively at schools.

Schools are now deciding the form of instruction for the 2020-21 school year. They're opting for hybrid or blended learning and exploring both synchronous and asynchronous learning.

Much is needed to make online learning work.

Schools will want to invest in meaningful professional development that helps teachers with the new tools and with pedagogy that explains how classroom management can work when students are not attending school in person. Teachers will want to explore social-emotional health and learning, build relationships with children who are not in the same space as them, and accept a different partnership with parents.

- ▶ **School Leadership Committee Takeaway**
  - ○ You can't do everything, at least not at once. You've gone through the chapters, discussed what they contained, reviewed, and answered the takeaway questions at the end. Now you have a lot to think about.
    - The major learnings from the educators interviewed, in priority order, were:
      - Food Insecurity/Digital Equity needed addressing quickly
      - Social-Emotional Health was a major concern
      - Leadership needed to set the right tone to steer the school

- Relationships were key
- Communication had to be frequent, meaningful, and interactive
- Online Learning and Teachers Stepping Up needed time and support
- Cybersecurity and Privacy were essential
- Infrastructure needed to support this style of instruction
- Parents had a new respect for teachers but struggled
- Schedules had to change
- Students showed resilience
- Thinking of your school, how will you prioritize your findings?
  - Are you in Online Learning now for the long haul?
  - Will you become a 1-to-1 school for every student, and support those who cannot afford a device and/or connectivity?
  - What type of ongoing professional development will occur now?
    - How will it address pedagogy?
    - How will it address tools?
    - Who will conduct the sessions?
    - How will you assess its usefulness?
  - How will the schedule change now that at least some learning is online?
    - Recalling the lessons from educators, you cannot replicate your usual schedule and put teachers and students together in front of screens for hours at a time. It's not healthy physically or mentally.
  - How will students be part of your plan moving forward? Hopefully, you have some students on your committee.
  - How will you involve parents?
  - Will you survey your stakeholders as part of your work together?

- What do you wish happened differently from March to the end of the school year?
    - How can you make those things happen now?
- The actual interviews follow. They are inspiring and authentic stories from the front line and will resonate with many.

Chapter 10 – Interviews

Introduction

It's my pleasure to present the interviews with the educational professionals who shared their stories of leading during COVID-19. Every conversation reinforced the main elements of this book; these elements became the content of the book chapters. Nearly every educator identified social-emotional health as a prime goal of getting their schools and districts through the extraordinary time of COVID-19. Most educators identified social-emotional health as their top worry. Keeping relationships healthy was another theme. Equity, food for children, ways to respect signature events and rituals, communication, and community were identified as other essential elements of school. And, to a person, every educator praised teachers who stepped up during extraordinary circumstances.

The Interviewees

The interviewees were a mixture of former colleagues from my days in schools, referrals from trusted colleagues and friends, and referrals from interviewees. There were educators from public, independent, Catholic, and international schools. Educators came from rural and city schools, small and medium-sized districts, schools with varying levels of funding, several U.S. states, and countries around the world, including Canada, Japan, Taiwan, and Turkey.

Yet the more educators were different, the more they were the same. All were concerned about student health, continuity of learning, and teacher support. Many understood parents were trying their best to offer a productive learning environment while they themselves were either working at home or experiencing unemployment. A good percentage of the interviewees were parents of school-age children trying to balance their instructional days with supporting their children's learning.

The common thread throughout this book was what happened during the COVID-19 crisis. However, any crisis that closed school for a length of time would require the same elements identified in this book. Attention to social-emotional health, ways to keep relationships going, addressing food insecurity and other equity issues, attention to cyber safety, and protecting privacy were all needed during this or any other crisis.

Why School?

You may notice that some of the interviewees wondered what school continuity means when you can't be in the same space at the same time. So many things are missing when school buildings are closed. Community, relationships, social-emotional health, food, and nurturance are necessary components in a school.

Themes, Learnings

What can be learned from these interviews are presented in Chapter 2 – Learnings.

Organization of Chapter

The interviews that follow are grouped by type of school or organization.

Public School Interviews

Victoria Andrews
Director of Technology and Innovation
Payson Unified School District, Payson AZ

Ms. Andrews' concern for her rural Arizona school district while school was closed was around communication, making sure children were fed, and accommodating students without digital access. When the school closed suddenly, and when students relied on meals in schools five days a week, not having food became the crisis. She says, "We offered meals for all students 18 years or younger whether they go to our school district or not. We provided mobile breakfast and lunch, with 7 or 8 bus routes with drivers going out with breakfast and lunch. The bus drivers would stay at each route til the designated announced time."

Another loss to solve at Payson Unified was Internet connectivity. Statistics say 7 out of 10 teachers have assigned homework via the Internet according to research from the Aspen Group https://www.aspeninstitute.org/blog-posts/the-homework-gap/#:~:text=Today%2C%20as%20many%20as%207,call%20it%20the%20Homework%20Gap [47].

But some students had neither devices nor Internet access at home. Like other schools, Payson pointed network access points towards areas students can visit. "We're opening schools in multiple areas with parking lots," says Ms. Andrews.

Andrews' team included student academic achievement teachers to provide Professional Development for teachers. Remote teaching was a different animal, and even if teachers had tried to deliver instruction this way before, it's unlikely they had instructed online over weeks or even months. And teachers who opted out of technology-infused instruction had few other methods to reach students. *"Everyone has to learn how to use tools. Even if it's not their cup of tea, they understand the need,"* said Andrews. Teachers at Payson adapted, delivered instruction differently, and collaborated.

---

47 Rosenworcel, Jessica. The Aspen Institute. *Millions of children can't do their homework because they don't have access to broadband internet.* June 30, 2016. accessed August 15, 2020.

Still, it was stressful for students, teachers, parents, and administrators. Everyone missed each other when they had to stay home. The social-emotional health of everyone at Payson was top of the mind for Andrews. But students coped with this unusual method of instruction. *"All the love that's there. It's amazing for some classes – high schools – you'd think they wouldn't make as much of an effort. They are there. Maybe they're working on a back field with a bulldozer but stopping to get on a call."*

Ms. Andrews speculated on what life might be like for students who have gone through COVID and experienced this emergency, *"Part of me is sad for them…"* She continued thinking about *"my son and his friends that age – I don't think they have felt the loss yet because key moments haven't happened. Kudos to them, they are putting on their brave face. There will be disappointment."*

Ms. Andrews continued, *"For my senior, he is looking to next steps to get accepted next fall. Will he be able to start school in fall, will the program be there? For him, he has a great attitude. He's traveled extensively and moved across the country. He's good at adjusting. That doesn't mean there won't be some heartbreak."*

She continues, *"I'm hoping the anxiety has quelled a little. And people come into new routines today. Maybe it's not so horrible because of team interactions. I'm hoping kids will adjust. They will remember that the world panicked and bought toilet paper. There are five cousins in Italy I talk with. I said, 'People want all the toilet paper.' Her response was 'Mamma mia.'"*

When asked what she'd tell other schools going through emergency remote learning, Ms. Andrews says, *"Do the best you can. My entire school did this all at once. It's like snowflakes, something is right for one, not for others. We did handouts. Some districts already had 1-to-1 and did it. And it's about being successful in the digital classroom. Some schools tried to just get devices out to students. We elected to stay the course until the next school year. We couldn't do other things if we prioritized 1-to-1. You still can be successful."*

Suzy Brooks
Director of Instructional Technology for Mashpee Public Schools, Mashpee MA
President of Massachusetts ASCD Affiliate
Co-Author of "Modern Mentor" part of the Lead Forward series, Times 10 Publications

Following the trend from interviewees at other schools, Ms. Brooks was proud of Mashpee teachers. *"Teachers have to step up, technology-wise. They become troubleshooters, tech support for their families. I'm really proud of teachers."* Ms. Brooks and her team made sure they supported teachers delivering emergency instruction. *"Every day an hour in the morning is tech therapy on Zoom, teachers can drop in, commiserate, ask for what is needed. We want to make it hard to be disconnected."*

She continued to describe some of the needs at Mashpee. *"There are some students who need more help and are of concern. Maybe these students are not living with parents, are with other relatives or have other challenges."* She continued that the solution was *"… a lot of outreach. The high school has called every family in the district to see if they have connectivity and need anything and if their Chromebook was working."* Making individual calls and not emails or automated calls was intentional. It's essential to have *"… human to human contact,"* Ms. Brooks said.

Continuing in communication vein, Ms. Brooks said communication had to be regular and more frequent than when school was open. Some students stopped participating, so they asked the counseling office to make calls. They didn't want to have seven or eight repeated requests to families. They didn't want to swamp parents. Mashpee understood that parents are in the trenches too. *"Parents more active whether they want to or not."*

When asked what this might mean to students now and in the future, Ms. Brooks emphasized children's ability to roll with changes. *"It's harder on us as adults. The kids will be fine. This is their reality; this is going to be their normal.*

For us adults, nothing is normal. Kids will roll with it. If this is something that can happen every year or couple of years in schools, it will take a lot more professional development and flexibility of space and time. It's hardest on people who had never fathomed this. Kids will be okay. They'll have something to tell their kids."

MaryEllen Bunton
Director of Curriculum
Danville District 118, Danville IL

At Ms. Bunton's district, the highest priority was making sure students were fed. When you relied on one or two meals daily five days a week, and suddenly this stopped, the lack of food became the most significant crisis. "Highest priority was we made sure kids were fed. We're a high needs district. Kids rely on getting food."

Remote emergency learning happened suddenly. Ms. Bunton shared, *"They didn't leave school knowing they wouldn't come back. Students didn't take things home with them. They didn't have materials."* A secondary issue was computers. Ms. Bunton said, *"Some kids only had phones. They had no Internet."*

Delivering instruction had to be considered. The program was called "Sharpening Skills at Home." Packets were put together for all levels from primary to secondary and included art and PE. Ms. Bunton described the instruction as *"No tech/low tech."* The goals were to try to think differently about learners and the community and to keep the learning going.

When asked about successes, Ms. Bunton gave glowing marks to district employees and the community. *"Foodservice workers gave their PPE to the hospital, so we used social media to say food service and custodial staff don't have any masks – is there anyone who can help? The response from the community was overwhelming. The biggest success story is the community. It's why we moved here. People were coming together."* Another positive was the *"time and space that teachers have been given to learn technology."*

Danville District is thinking about teaching and learning for the next school year. They are examining what students should master and what they haven't practiced enough to master during remote emergency learning. An analysis of the remote learning that happened during COVID-19 will be turned over to the teachers for the next school year. *"We need all summer to get teachers on board. There would be more professional development if the next school year involved hybrid or completely virtual learning."* How the school will return in 2020-21 was unknown as of the time of the interview.

Ms. Bunton provided some thoughtful perspectives on the fallout from everyone going through this remote emergency learning crisis together. *"What might be different is that the teaching profession is revered again. People see the importance of it. Teachers were doing the best for kids and the community and were legislated to death. Not everyone can be a teacher. We need to love on [teachers]. It's a critical job."*

Ms. Bunton continued, *"As for students, kids really understand what has been taken away from them. Education is something they are so used to, but it is critical to growing up. Equity is around tech, but there are also other significant equity issues like electricity, food, and water. It's so important to see each other. Taking care of each other helps to make learning happen."*

She continues, *"Things are getting more like they used to be when my kids were growing up. People are constantly walking by. Kids are in the park doing things. I hope this leads to a better balance. We've tried to make sure that no tech and tech work. Hopefully, the relationship piece is so important and not replaced by screens."*

As to advice to other schools going through emergency online learning, Ms. Bunton *says, "Give yourself some grace. Ask for it. Be patient with parents, kids, and staff. There's a post that's been going around that someone is talking about Building Apollo 13. Like then, we had 24 hours to do a 360 with instruction. We did it. Give yourself some grace. Ask for grace from the community. Understand that we've got the power to help ease some of the stress. We don't have to create more stress; we have the power to make it less stressful. See the perspective – technology is critical – but relationships are needed to get things accomplished. Make sure you have relationships with the union, with parents, stakeholders, each other, with the administration group at the district level. When one person needs a minute, pick up the slack, work as a team. The rest will come."*

John Case
Director of Technology
Ohio Hi-Point Career Center, Bellefontaine OH

Mr. Case and his team initially tried to figure out which students had Internet access, and which did not. Given the emergency nature of school closing, this became a priority even though there is a 1-to-1 laptop program for students at Ohio Hi-Point. When parks, McDonald's, Starbucks, libraries, and the other places were closed, students could no longer rely on these places for free Wi-Fi.

Hi-Point's primary challenge was communication. They wanted to figure out how to make sure everyone stayed in touch and knew the plan, where to get resources, and what was needed. All this happened during an emergency.

When asked what he'd share with other schools, Mr. Case said, *"We told our staff that this is triage, not the everyday norm. We don't expect to be experts at everything. Try and give your best. Use the support system in place. Our supervisors are great. People have places to turn. "*

Mike Daugherty
Director of Technology & Innovation
Chagrin Falls Exempted Village Schools, Chagrin Falls, OH

Mr. Daugherty started by praising his teachers as they adapted during a period of emergency remote learning. *"I love seeing teachers connecting on Meet or Zoom with kids. Teachers did an amazing job. From our surveys, teachers said one-on-one interaction was what they missed. The majority of our teachers are doing virtual classrooms or one-on-one. They're coming up with really engaging lessons. If we said we were going to do this, it would have been a three-year initiative. I can't say enough about what teachers have done."*

As to challenges, Mr. Daugherty shared, *"I live in this world. Now we're educating my three kids from home. The workload and how things are being managed need to be adapted to each kid's personality. It's the new normal."* As to other parents, Mr. Daugherty said, *"We wrapped up a survey on Tues. Some results showed parents saying the workload is overwhelming; you need to step back and slow down. Other parents say if my student is done by 11 a.m., it's not good enough. Some parents are clamoring for more activities and instruction, some saying it's too much. Some parents say we should have an eight to three schedule, Zoom meeting after Zoom meeting, like a normal class day. All in all, feedback is very positive."*

Responding to a question about advice to other schools, Daugherty offered *"Hang in there and do your best. It's such a different time now. The community, parents, students all understand this is a new norm for now. Do what you can, continue to be what you can. Do your best. You can't solve every problem for every student. Keep students at the center."*

William Fritz
Director of Technology at Sycamore Community Schools, Cincinnati OH
Executive Director of Learn21

Mr. Fritz framed the work at Sycamore Community Schools as learning continuity. *"We're trying to do a continuity plan. We started right away to begin remote learning, not knowing how long it will last. It's a moving target. We settled in to calling this a remote learning continuity plan."*

As to success stories, Mr. Fritz pointed first to teachers. *"We are seeing some great success stories with teachers. They are understanding how to make the shift, really doing a good job. They know how to manage time, not thinking I must meet students at eight at the first bell. They are really recognizing how to use tools asynchronously. We decided it's not like we need to go to every bell."*

Asked about challenges, Mr. Fritz shared, *"Teachers were never prepared for remote learning. Ideally, you ought to have three versions of learning: face-to-face, blended, and online. I said, wouldn't it be nice to require an online section of a class? Before this, they all looked like I was crazy when talking about these three versions. My dad said one person could make it any way they want, but masses require consistency to sustain the environment. Go ahead for yourself; for others, you need consistency. Teachers are now more prepared to teach this way."*

As to students who lived through the closing of school for an emergency, Mr. Fritz mentioned his own three sons. *"My sons are 27, 24, and the 18-year-old is a senior. He plays sports but not now. There will be no graduation ceremony. The COVID Kids. People name generations."*

He continued reflecting on students. *"I believe they have been fed up with testing. All these things were thrown at them; my son is numb to it all a bit. He's not caught up yet. Reality – really? Are we done with school? There are whisperings of a staggered start in fall. Some parents might not let children come back yet. This generation – in a shadow of COVID – will not remember the same things as others. I wonder how important college graduation will be for them. They'll have a bond too. They'd say, 'I was a 2020 grad.' Maybe they'll have their own following. A book out there about it might have a hashtag #2020."*

Mr. Fritz suggested some ideas for other schools going through emergency learning. *"Keep it simple. Meaning simple for tools, delivery, and for not introducing anything new for teachers. Teachers are good at what they do already. If you push new tools they've never used before, it causes a lot of stress and angst. That's not successful at all. Teachers were pretty stressed about keeping up. Tell them they have got to work together with technology and educational leadership. Create a continuity plan. Create a contingency plan. Stress transcendence. Go to the next level after this. Maybe take every Monday off and give teachers a breather. Both synchronous and asynchronous learning are needed."*

Mr. Fritz continued, *"Have a plan. Schools should have that plan that they revisit one day a month. There should be an eLearning day scheduled. Work with community leaders, parents, staff, admin, and put in the due process on the contingency plan once a month. Don't think it will be one and done."*

Jennifer Fry
Chief Technology Officer
Delaware City Schools, Delaware OH

Ms. Fry described the process at Delaware City Schools when it became clear schools needed to close quickly. The leadership team started putting together a teaching and learning plan for what might happen. They did not know what was coming, so planned for multiple scenarios. Teachers would have to implement the district LMS even if they hadn't used it before.

Ms. Fry explained initial plans *"went out the window quickly once we realized school was going to close, so we went to Plan C. School closed, and students moved to remote learning. We created a document and called it the Flexible Learning Plan. This included having teachers work from the district LMS, Canvas, which had been the learning platform for six years. The LMS was not new for most, but teacher use was never mandated."*

The LMS would be mandated now. *"We moved to common expectations of how many minutes of work was to be created at each grade level. We shared resource lists for teachers. We shared district tech tools and links. There were common expectations and support. We were to have a PD (Professional Development) day, which was supposed to be a celebratory day to showcase practices, and it was all planned."* The day was wholly changed, given the need for all teachers to learn remote learning.

When asked about success stories, Ms. Fry described how teachers stepped up. *"Our elementary teachers weren't using the LMS before this and never had a vision of how to use it, and now they got thrown into a situation. They didn't complain and have been so creative and used exciting ways to connect to kids. Kindergarten teachers shared reading lessons. It was unbelievable. If I had been the parent, what a window this would have been into the classroom."*

Ms. Fry continued praising the teachers working during COVID-19 remote learning, *"The courage that this takes. Teachers haven't complained or fussed. It's real success. In the education technology world, it's hard, but some of the things we have worked for with blended and personalized learning are happening now. It's the most bang for the buck in two months' time. We have to be sure not to let them slide back. Blended and personalized learning is an expectation. So long to old habits."* Ms. Fry describes it as a silver lining to the emergency learning implemented. *"It's some good to take away."*

This extraordinary time impacted students. Ms. Fry reflected on remote emergency learning, *"I have a senior in high school. He doesn't think it's such a big deal. He's getting ready to go to college and won't even have typical college experiences. Everything will be impacted. These seniors have had a very different end of the senior year - no graduation and an e-porch prom. Some don't care. Some of them really care."*

When asked about advice to other schools, Ms. Fry says, *"The thing that I've been most proud about in our school district is that we worked collaboratively as a team and put forward consistent communications for teachers, community, and parents. We've really tried to have a plan the entire time."*

Patrick Hausammann
Supervisor of Instructional Technology/ITRT (Instructional Technology Resource Teacher)
Clarke County Public Schools, Berryville VA

Success stories for Mr. Hausammann started with teachers. *"I'm excited and happy about the collaboration that has been spurred by the close with respect to reaching out to other teachers. Teachers are working smarter, not harder. Several of us from the ITRT group built sites for teachers with content. Administrators forwarded resources to add."*

Another area of pride in Clarke County's response, Mr. Hausamman said, was *"… communication across the board, constant communication. Google Meet, phone* calls, emails, messenger apps. At no point did the community (students, staff, and guardians) feel not informed."

Challenges for Mr. Hausammann included equity issues. "A big challenge is equity - students that don't have devices or connectivity. We are trying to give instruction equitably, but what about students who can't stream in? Another challenge is special education populations in remote learning atmospheres."

He saw teachers adapt to remote learning. "At least a couple of teachers who had normally been tiptoeing and not jumping in—who were not as comfortable—have gotten onboard with 1-to-1 and not just using packets. They're going digital and collaborating with peers to create rich learning experiences."

Asked about the historical perspective of closed schools and what this might mean for students, Mr. Hausammann speculated, "When 9/11 happened, I thought, 'Is this something for history books now?' Students may have the same thoughts living in an historical moment that has never happened before. Teachers cannot remember a closure of this mass. This will be remembered in a negative way for some. There was no graduation across the stage, no college visits for some—it's all just virtual. But there are positives. I hope history books say kids and teachers learned how to do something in a different way, collaboration rose, some families grew closer, we innovated instead of stagnating, and the other positive impacts including information literacy for students."

As to some advice for other schools, Mr. Hausammann offered, "The number one thing: start small and don't feel you have to recreate the wheel. There are a ton of resources and ed-tech companies; no need to jump into all those things. Think about the tools and things you are using already. Make little changes. Start with where the gaps are and plan from there. Is a tool missing to fill the content or allow students to do something?"

He continued, "Connecting to that is ramping up or reinforcing collaboration and communication. Try to get teachers connected to virtual faculty and team meetings, so no one feels they are in this by themselves, and they don't go back to the silos *that characterized education years ago. Get people the resources they need. Don't overwhelm them. Support starts small, case-by-case as they need it. Don't send out two hundred links on a list of resources and expect teachers to have at it. Reach out on social media, speak to other districts. Be informed and pinpoint your support."*

Mr. Hausammann recommended reaching out to other educators. *"One of the great things at the district level in Virginia is that we started using #GoOpenVA (a state Open Education Resource hub from the state department of education) and a number of schools have posted plans, resources and more to that platform. People are putting up resources freely and seeking collaboration outside the boundaries of our district. Great to see. Even at the district level, walls started to come down. We'd already launched in January – it happened to be just before we needed it. Social media, professional learning networks, and organizations (like VSTE, ISTE, etc.) are all great places to seek resources, collaboration, and honest feedback."*

Monty Hitschler
Director of Information Services and Technologies
Town of Rockport and Rockport Public Schools, Rockport MA

Mr. Hitschler shared successes at Rockport Public Schools. *"My wife was telling me about some success today. She is the Prek-12 math coordinator in the district. She said It's forcing teachers and those co-teaching to focus on a single subject instead of multiple subjects. As a district, we've been pleased with attendance by kids as high as 100%, not sure it will stay. We hear kids say they are very excited to see classmates. The equipment, training, software we've purchased previously has paid off."*

As to challenges, the district wanted to be sure every student had a working device, and for online learning to succeed. They wanted to ensure *"equitable access, for every kid"* according to Mr. Hitschler. They found sometimes they didn't have the right contact information for families, and sometimes they received no response. The need for accurate family information was clear.

The budget was allocated differently during this emergency, which will impact next year's budget. However, changes will continue. Rockport Public Schools were

1-to-1, but students did not take computers home. That changed during this crisis and will remain that way in the future. Devices will stay with students at home.

Attendance was challenging. Mr. Hitschler says, *"How do you count days off? Massachusetts is not counting attendance for the rest of the year. We try to keep track of attendance, but can you really?"*

As to what students might remember or embrace about going through an extraordinary time, Mr. Hitschler shared a story from his own family. *"I have a 13-year-old, and when they closed the schools down, she turned to me and said 'This is the first thing that I'm going to remember that was a major event that I'm going to tell my kids and see in the history books.'"* He continued to describe what students are going through. *"They can't wait to see friends. Seniors, proms, parties missed. Personal celebrations or just a pat on the back, it's all not happening."*

Comparing the COVID-19 crisis with another major world event, Mr. Hitschler said, *"9/11 changed things, but this will have a bigger impact longer. Economically what will be left? Are we only doing online takeout? Will there be no little stores, no JC Penney? We received an actual note from my wife's nephew and thought this is how people used to communicate in olden times. A light went off in my wife's head. We are all going to remember this."*

Advice from Mr. Hitschler to other schools included, *"Make sure all your data is right; it's hard to get ahold of people if you don't have the right phone numbers and emails. You will need to practice remote learning regularly. Flip the classroom, do a regular training program. Maybe there's a half-day when students go home, and everyone (students/teachers) has the rest of the day working from home."*

Jeanne Knouse
Director of Student Services
State College Area School District, State College PA

Ms. Knouse discussed what happened at State College Area School District during the coronavirus pandemic.

"If we didn't have spring break in March, we might not have shut down. There was so much virus in the U.S. at the time," she shared. Ms. Knouse continued, *"There was a discussion during spring break about what remote learning might look like. We thought it would be for a week or two. That grew to the whole rest of the school year."*

She described the demographics at State College, a college town where Pennsylvania State University's main campus is located, as having a *"high need population and a low need population."* They surveyed the community to determine the new needs brought on by the pandemic. Many people were laid off or had lost their jobs altogether. The district staff moved quickly to needs and support assessment. She continued, *"The community wanted to donate money to help others."* Ms. Knouse immediately thought of SCASD's Education Foundation. Ms. Knouse and other staff had done a fundraiser previously and raised $50K for training, mental health services, and programs. Ms. Knouse and her team were planning to spend $15K of that to educate the community, staff, and kids on mental health issues. They thought perhaps families in the district could donate money towards this fund.

Instead, the community pleasantly surprised Ms. Knouse and the district staff by donating $106K.

Next, Ms. Knouse and her team decided to purchase gift cards in $100 increments. They reached out to families and assessed their needs. They distributed the gift cards in three levels--three hundred dollars per family, two hundred, and one hundred. Food was the most critical need in the community. She said, *"To date, we have given $25K in food assistance and $5K for rent and bills. We also used $5K to create integrated mental health kits."*

It became an all hands on deck effort. Ms. Knouse and her team were able to deputize some Pennsylvania State University psychology students to help make calls to families and assist with the assessment process. The assessment process helped not only the school district, but the Penn State students themselves; the University allowed students to stop attending classes because of the pandemic but had not released them from graduation requirements. One requirement was to have an internship in their field. Students participating in the SCASD process earned their internship credit and, in some cases, did not have to repeat an entire year of college.

Ms. Knouse was appointed to coordinate the district COVID-19 response. She had a special education and restorative practices background and led a team of counselors and nurses. The social-emotional health of the community benefitted. Ms. Knouse and her team implemented trauma practices and planned lessons for the upcoming school year. One essential program was called Restorative Practices. She explained, *"Engagement, explanation, expectation are key components of Restorative Practices. When I'm engaged, you're getting my thoughts, and then I gave you an expectation."* Ms. Knouse continued, *"Maybe that didn't feel fair because you're telling me something, but you didn't engage me with that, you just told me."* The staff was practiced using Restorative Practices all summer.

Specific populations were challenged more than others. Special education students and multidisciplinary classes need hands-on work. Parents had to take over managing learning from home. She elaborated, "Teachers felt useless because they couldn't help struggling kids." Ms. Knouse wondered about the upcoming school year after the pandemic outbreak. SCASD had planned to return to in-person classes. *"How do you physically distance kids? There's no leniency from the state as to getting things done. We are putting people at risk. Immune suppressed kids. Some won't be wearing a mask because their disabilities mean they can't remove a mask. The CDC recommends if you can't remove a mask yourself, you can't wear a mask."*

Diversity is a factor at SCASD partly in terms of languages spoken and also because of economic struggles. State College Area School District students speak 37 languages. Some non-English speaking families worked in local restaurants but lost their jobs due to COVID-19. "We had a translation bank of people willing to help the families. We had Spanish teachers and interpreters help out."

SCASD had to communicate with the families and students and overcome the language barrier while helping with economic stress.

Ms. Knouse explained how more people pitched in to help with the language barriers and with resources. *"A retired teacher started a grassroots food and diaper distribution for economically struggling families. There was massive community support."* The close relationship with Pennsylvania State University also helped. *"Using the Pennsylvania State University World Languages Department for translation helped us to connect families with services,"* explained Ms. Knouse.

When asked about how the pandemic will impact this generation of children going through the COVID-19 crisis, Ms. Knouse shared, *"They have a story to tell. Life is not the same right now, but it's your experience. Mask wearing will probably happen. Immuno-suppressed people should have been wearing masks all along."* She continued, *"My daughter is 20 and in college, and she's like the COVID police. These kids won't leave the house without a mask. They've become smarter; they're washing their hands, they're social and physically distancing. They're wearing masks."*

Dr. Mike Muir
Learning through Technology Director
MSAD 44, Bethel ME

Dr. Muir shared his perspective on this extraordinary time with schools closed, *"This is not online education. This is emergency learning at a distance. There's the sense that this is emergency – not online learning. It doesn't meet standards for online learning. So many vital components for learning, especially for hard-to-teach kids, are almost all missing from online learning platforms. Online learning platforms offer nothing about relationships, sparking kids, reframing connections, connecting student lives to the real world."*

Dr. Muir said they are working on *"… online communications to families while we do our best to do something that looks like learning."*

Taking a view of what opportunities exist during this extraordinary time, Dr. Muir begins, *"How do we marry what we learned from what is working and isn't working and turn this into professional development support for the next level? Just to synthesize what works and doesn't without direct support modeling educational resources would be insane."*

He continued, *"How do we get the people who think they know all the answers but know very little to stay out of our hair? Some things are harmful. Some foundations have a long history of doing things and walking away."*

Dr. Muir also pointed out another opportunity and said, *"There's nothing like a national health crisis to put a glaring spotlight on digital inequality. We're lucky that in Maine we are 1-to-1 for grades 7 and 8. In Bethel, unlike some Maine districts, we are 1-to-1 for all students K-12. We have ideas on how to teach with technology and also provide coaching for teachers."*

"Still," he adds, *"there are a lot of kids who don't have devices. 1-to-1 programs are not all created equal. Some districts are buying the cheapest Chromebook available. Nothing becomes more expensive than an inexpensive device that doesn't do what you want. It's better to spend more on a device that does what you want it to."*

A big issue is *"… Internet at home. What Angus King termed the 'homework divide.' Angus King is the Governor that started 1-to-1 in Maine. We were surprised by how some parents did not have Wi-Fi. The state is now working to provide hot spots. They are Using CARES funds to bring devices to people who need them."*

Another opportunity, Dr. Muir says, is *"We have to figure out how to implement in an online way or never be successful."* He lists some of the critical things to consider: *"1. Relationships with kids 2. Connect learning to kids' lives and the real world 3. Help kids to see how knowledge is useful and interesting 4. Figure out what kids know and understand to build in 5. Identify misperceptions and gaps to moving forward 6. Make learning hands-on. "*

Dr. Muir says there's a need to *"Create a platform where you can design a project of interest, connect to standards, access resources, and background and have conversations with teachers."*

Asked for advice for schools going through this extraordinary time, Dr. Muir said, *"People started compiling huge lists of resources. It was hard work they did lovingly to try to help teachers. Instead, it's best to minimize how much I gave them. Create a teacher resource page and a parent resource page. In the beginning, it was just curating one or two good articles on getting Zoom set up, so they don't have to Google and find things. Things like how to fix the audio. Best to share three or four things they'll really have problems with. Deliberately we wanted not to overwhelm teachers."*

Other advice Dr. Muir gave was, *"Just be available. Teachers reach out to key technicians or me. Help parents and families."*

Dr. Muir continued, *"Teachers' efforts to reach kids have been extraordinary. We had to give permission to teachers to stop at 3 or 4 p.m. Some parents are available only in the evening. We encouraged teachers to take their time back."*

Dr. Muir was asked about the future impact of online learning. He said, *"How education will be changed may be too strong a paradigm. I don't know a lot will change. There are three things with an opportunity now to change 1. Adequate learning devices. Not every device is adequate yet. 2. Homework gap – solving the broadband issue. It's a socio-economic solution that's needed. Equity in access. 3. This crisis highlighted how traditional teaching isn't adequate to motivate kids to put the time in. There need to be conditions for self-motivation. It's NOT just compliance. What motivates underachieving kids? There's some talk about motivation and what they really mean is compliance. How do we create conditions for self-motivation? 3.B. – Karen Cator (Digital Promise) and the learning divide – the quality of learning experiences that different kids get needs to be addressed. Passive learning vs. active learning. There is very much a racial and socioeconomic divide. Equity of learning experiences is needed. A hope to provide equally high-quality learning experiences. We put low-performing students with the most boring and worst teachers."*

Arline Pique
Director of Technology
Hamilton County Educational Service Center, Cincinnati OH

Ms. Pique offered some reflections on remote emergency learning with schools closed. *"We are all feeling isolated and, at the same time, better connected because of the online tools available. The stars are aligning with technology and allowing us to connect. We're having more face-to-face meetings with our teams and with other people, even across states."*

She explained, *"Districts were very competitive. Now it's a different story. Everyone is thinking about how to pull it all together. This emergency is beyond a snow day. Now we're trying to think about ramifications for the next school year on how to do well together and become stronger."*

She described some human stories of school during COVID-19. *"One of my teammates wears a goofy hat costume during video meetings to make everyone chuckle. A friend who is a seamstress makes masks for people. She's not making any money from the masks. During video conferences, we are getting a glimpse into each other's homes. We are finding out this is the way my house looks. I've seen team members' kids and their spouses. Our superintendent ran a meeting that kicked off with a song that represented a time he was emotional, and his wife put her head on his shoulder. Those pictures in our minds will be framed forever."*

Thinking of students going through this extraordinary time, Ms. Pique shared, *"I do think that these students used to dread going to school. Now they really appreciate school when we don't have school. They're feeling like going through COVID-19 will give them an appreciation of what they have at the moment, and they will stop thinking about things they used to take for granted."*

She reflected on a previous crisis many people went through and its impact. *"After 9/11, everyone had flags in the car, and I wondered at the time how long there would be the flag in vehicles. The flags disintegrated. Then no one else had flags in their cars."*

Ms. Pique said, *"This time reminds me of the generation after the Great Depression. Our grandparents were either saving or spending because they lost so much. The Great Depression forever impacted that generation."*

She said, *"This generation will be forever changed by COVID-19."*

Ms. Pique continued, *"After 9/11, my dad told my 11-year old daughter he was 10 when Pearl Harbor happened. He had her sit on his lap and said, 'Mark this time in your head, your grandchildren will want to hear about it.' These children will have stories to tell their grandchildren."*

As to what she might tell other schools going through such an extraordinary time, Ms. Pique said, *"We're learning a lot on how to transform and what comes next. We have been talking about innovation, changing school to be that place kids want to be, in charge of learning, where they have a voice. But we're running into compliance testing and red tape. We are Innovating right now in a way we could never do before. It's an incredible opportunity for moving forward and not going back. It's how to make innovation happen. "*

She added, *"We're seeing inequities that government and business can't ignore. We realize that "busy" was our enemy. Relationships with families and students and parents and teachers are one of the most important things we can ever have. What matters is connection with each other. Students crave this proximity to each other."*

Annamaria Schrimpf
Director of Educational Technology and Digital Learning
Shawsheen Valley Technical District, Billerica MA

Ms. Schrimpf shared what happened at Shawsheen Valley Technical District when the coronavirus forced schools to close, *"Our Principal has put out guidelines. We're to connect once a week with students. We are to keep staying connected with students. Also, we share resources for the curriculum areas. We're not 1-to-1 yet but hoping so in the future. We reached out to the student population to see if they need devices. We made devices available if they were needed. Many students didn't need devices."* She *emphasized, "The key was to stay connected to our students."*

Ms. Schrimpf shared success stories from her district, *"Under these unfortunate circumstances, teachers are using the technology and exploring how to be successful. Administrators can video conference. It's exciting for teachers, even though it's hard at times. Teachers have been very professional. They are really learning systems. We are working under constraints; we have to keep up with state requirements. A lot of teachers were using technology tools in such a short amount of time. Teachers Just jumped right in and rolled up their sleeves."*

Thinking of challenges, Ms. Schrimpf shared, *"There are a lot of free resources. We need to be cautious. Data privacy issues exist. Resources will go away after this emergency. Zoom has been offered for free, which is great. But if teachers have something like Zoom, we encourage them. Eventually, Zoom will require payment. Companies are smart to market their products as free right now. Educators have to be cautious unless we plan to purchase; the products may have to go away."*

Considering this unique time for schools and sharing advice, Mr. Schrimpf said, *"We have to reflect during this time. COSN did research and found that over half of schools have 1-to-1 devices. We have to figure out how to get devices in the hands of all students. Students have smartphones but are not doing 'mindful tasks.' We need to take away that students need to understand how to use these devices beyond personal use. "*

She continued, saying much of the usage by students of devices was doing *"… mindless tasks although they stay connected with their friends. Educators need to be reflective of how education technology plays an instrumental role. My school district realizes the importance of putting a spotlight on learning. Engage in more planning, support, and understanding."* She recommended planning should be *"… not about the devices. We should support the classroom, lead co-teaching with education technology."*

Todd Wesley
Chief Technology Office
Lakota Local School District, Liberty/West Chester Townships OH

Mr. Wesley describes what is being done at the Lakota Local School District to address remote emergency learning. *"While instruction is central, so many things are required for learning. First and foremost, is proper nutrition for our students. Our Child Nutrition team has done an amazing job mobilizing resources to provide thousands of meals to any children in need in our community both at designated pickup locations and at drop-offs since schools have been closed."*

He continued, *"Next, students need to feel a connection to their learning, which is one of the biggest challenges of remote learning. Our teachers have really stepped up and embraced this challenge, beginning the process with calling our students, creating videos for their students, and scheduling virtual meetups."*

Mr. Wesley shared, *"As for student learning, we are blessed with having an established, personalized learning initiative purposefully supported by technology, called WE are EMPOWERED, based on the ISTE standards and Future Ready Schools model already in place. Thankfully, this includes many of the required approaches, resources, teacher supports, and leadership needed to support remote learning. "*

He continued, *"Our student feedback has shown that the most positive part of remote learning is their 'Ability to work at their own pace and schedule.'"*

He added, *"Our teachers have organized several activities and projects that support social emotional health, community outreach and even a district-wide spirit wear week. Our teachers are very focused on developing the whole child, remote or not and our teachers, staff and especially students continue to overcome the barriers and rise to the challenge. We all continue to learn a lot together along the way."*

As to success stories, Mr. Wesley replied, *"The work of our entire district and community to bring sudden remote learning to life is a success story on its own … I couldn't be prouder!"*

Mr. Wesley also said, *"I will say that our leadership team continued to follow the media reports on the virus, evaluated our preparedness for a remote shift, and proactively scheduled a Remote Learning Day Exercise. Similar to a safety exercise, this was designed to test the systems, teacher, student, and staff understanding of the usage and digital/remote approaches, as well as capacity."*

Mr. Wesley pointed to equity as a challenge, *"Digital equity has been the primary technology challenge. Our 7-12 students all have a district-issued laptop. However, our 3-6 students do not. We worked with our partners and converted our "in school" devices to take home, and our principals reached out and connected our students in need with the available devices. We also continue to promote our local internet provider Spectrum's offer for 60 days of free wireless internet to student homes in our community who are not current customers. We provide limited mobile internet hotspots to students who have no other option."*

Thinking of the impact of this global pandemic on children, Mr. Wesley listed possible changes. *"I anticipate there will be several takeaways from this sudden forced transition to remote learning and remote working globally. Anything from realizing the impact of the "overscheduled" lives we were all living and its impact on the family. Understanding what roles can be successfully done remotely and when face to face is critical. Realizing how so many more activities, both learning and professional, can be done asynchronously. A renewed discussion on new learning approaches, sciences and limiting hours and hours of homework, and possibly a new understanding of efficiencies through technology. That data will drive private and public sector trends and employee skills expectations, which in turn should drive changes in education."*

Ms. Wesley continued, *"I think a guiding question may ultimately be, once social distancing subsides, can this experience be used as a springboard to continue the remote approaches that worked, blended with the onsite approaches that worked, creating a truly flexible schedule to provide the ultimate personalization and empowerment for students and, frankly, some staff. Time will tell."*

As to advice to other schools going through a similar crisis, Mr. Wesley shared, *"In the recent words of Jon Bon Jovi, 'When you can't do what you do/ You do what *you can.' Every community, district and school have their own challenges. It's been inspiring to see so many education leaders, teachers, parents, grandparents, and students come together with businesses, hospitals, and governments to shift school to a remote model in a matter of days and finish the school year. I recommended expanded collaboration between districts. I'm part of a weekly statewide collaborative of EdTech Leaders and Instructional coaches, and each week the discussions of what is happening across the state of Ohio for students are so inspiring. It isn't perfect, but all we can do is our best right now and use this summer to assess, recalibrate, retool and re-approach these challenges in the fall as we move through these uncertain times!"*

Jeff Whipple
Digital Learning Lead
Anglophone School District–West, Fredericton, New Brunswick, Canada

Mr. Whipple explained how the Anglophone School District-West coped with closing during the COVID-19 crisis, *"I'm so impressed by our Minister of Education. He let science and policy speak rather than entertain emotional reactions. Like elsewhere in Canada, it's socialistic, not individualistic. The first three weeks were to focus on teachers, students, and families. We want to make sure kids are okay. We wanted to make sure families are okay. We didn't know where students were during the day. Teachers wanted to find out what to do, schools, and daycare were all closed. A few daycare centers were open to serve children of essential service workers, doctors, nurses, and firemen."*

Mr. Whipple continued, *"After those three weeks, a lot of smart people got together. They asked, 'What does school look like for us?' Any student in Grade 12 who has met minimal requirements will graduate. No additional requirements. Students who hadn't met the requirements will be given the opportunity 1-on-1 to build up credits. As of now, every Grade 12 student will graduate at the end of June."*

Mr. Whipple added, "We're calling this Continuation of Learning. The direction to teachers is to contact each family/student depending on age level and determine what is best for that family to continue. What do they need? I'm impressed with the professionals in our system."

Mr. Whipple said they decided, *"Lower grades would have no grading. Teachers provided learning opportunities for the whole class or individuals. For some with access to technology they could use technology, for some who may not know if they will have food on the table, it's hard to study and learn. "*

The goal was around social-emotional health. *"We meant to provide students with support through this time. The Ministry said the priority is emotional, psychological support. To hell with marks, make sure the kids are ok. Some kids need learning to take place. We had no expectation for students to do anything. I've been so impressed with how it's going."*

Thinking of challenges, Mr. Whipple said, *"We are working with all kinds of teachers, some like technology. Some don't. One teacher is a nice guy, but technology is not his thing. He probably uses mostly a whiteboard, and dry erase marker. He He called up on Friday night and said he needs help. He teaches middle school. I showed him Microsoft Teams and how to activate teams and how to send a simple message to his students. You would think he was shown the keys to paradise. He literally cried. Now he could interact with his students. "*

He continued, *"So this week he and I had another meeting, and this time he wanted to know how to do video conferencing. I showed him how, apparently, it had gone well. We are seeing teachers who before could ignore tech and had to be forced to use it—now they are in. Now they are stretching boundaries, stretching us. It's good for me professionally. I'm revitalizing the same thing for fifteen years, and it had become a little stagnant, but it's been fun helping teachers do something we should be doing. "*

As to what going through this crisis might mean to students now and in the future, Mr. Whipple said, *"I have a fear about graduating grade 12 students. I wonder what they are thinking. There are so many plans for graduation or prom or summer things. And now this has pulled so much out from under them. Our Minister reached out directly to grads through YouTube, Facebook, and other things. He was in his office with banners for 2020. He said, 'I don't know what graduation will look like for you. Congratulations, you are now a graduate.' It's not any less special.*

We will do something as a province so that every graduate remembers this as a special time.' He is very concerned. The program used to be called Kids Come First. Kids will remember this time off school."

Mr. Whipple's advice for going through an extraordinary crisis with schools closed was, *"Forget about marks, especially right now. Forget about testing; forget about trying to teach like you always taught. We have emergency outreach to our kids. That's what we are doing. Worry more about kids' emotional and physical well-being than about anything else. If they miss addition, teach it another time. For each kid, it's different. Some may need food in their home. Some kids get breakfast and lunch at school. Our food banks and community service and teachers have been outstanding to look after students. Worry about the kids and don't worry about the academics is the approach. Five years from now, ten years from now, it won't matter."*

Independent School Interviews

James Bologna
Director of Technology, Co-Director of Teaching & Learning, Global Academy Site Director
Windward School, Los Angeles CA

Mr. Bologna had glowing words for how his faculty responded to remote emergency learning. He said he has been *"constantly amazed at how faculty pivoted and adapted."* He described what was needed *"to ask the whole community to switch to virtual school mode. Both asynchronous and synchronous – it's a big shift."* Seeing Windward teachers make this shift, almost like being new teachers, he termed *"humbling."*

But the work was not without challenges. Mr. Bologna described some issues at Windward: *"We attempted to mirror our original schedule and found that it put a strain on faculty and students. We received a lot of feedback from students, families, teachers on having so much time on screen for school, plus time for socializing, and homework. It's too much." After* collecting feedback from the entire community, Windward adjusted the schedule for the sake of students, faculty, and parents.

Effective communication from the administration was vital to success at Windward School and improved during emergency learning. Mr. Bologna said, *"For students and families, our administration has shifted to a scheduled contact mode where the administrators divvied up families and reached out on a fairly regular basis to families. It's been going okay. Most are not having difficulties or just started getting online."*

Even though Mr. Bologna did not have a crystal ball to consult, he speculated, *"This hopefully tells us that we need to make some adjustments to the way we live. Once we address this pandemic, there's a likelihood of another high case count. Student lives are probably to become a blend of online activities and in-person activities. This will have an impact on their future. "*

His advice to other schools going through extraordinary emergency learning was, *"Keep up the good fight. You are not alone - we are all experiencing this to one degree or another. This situation presents a unique set of challenges that no one should have to deal with on their own. Reach out to your communities. You will find they are willing to help and share. Leverage your learning communities and the ISED newsgroups for the wealth of shared information and experiences. Education technologists and operational technologists have always been very generous with their time."*

Tye Campbell
Director of Technology
Gilman School, Baltimore MD

Mr. Campbell described elements that helped Gilman through remote emergency learning, especially around faculty and taking care of everyone. *"Be supportive of faculty. Consider it's been a challenge. We all have to acknowledge it has been a heavy lift, and this is not how they were trained to teach or to work with students. Classroom management is different than in person; it becomes difficult to judge where students are in terms of understanding. Teachers love to be masters in the classroom.*

It takes time to get used to learning as much as students and parents. Also, remember self-care. Remember to take care of families, balance all that."

When asked about success stories, Mr. Campbell focused on teachers. *"Some of our teachers who were nervous about using video conferences to teach, and some teachers who were not inclined to leverage an LMS (Learning Management System) have had to jump on it. They now recognize the value of the LMS as a tool to communicate with students and parents."* Remote emergency learning triggered some new reflections on instruction. Mr. Campbell continued, *"Teachers are thinking of assessment differently. Maybe a regular test is not the best way. They've assigned a lot of papers. What if a presentation were assigned instead? Teachers are thinking about how to make this more well-rounded. There are opportunities to speak publicly through Zoom - maybe we can help better shape learning experiences."*

As for challenges, Mr. Campbell talked about a problem that resulted in growth for Gilman teachers. *"It's important not to let perfect be the enemy of good. Teachers work incredibly hard. Teachers started spending hours making videos and editing them. It took them so long. One of the messages is that if you can't edit what you taught live, don't try to do it now. You make mistakes, just record yourself. Keep going. You're not expecting perfection from students. Don't expect it from yourself. By trying to be perfect, unnecessary pressure translates to kids. I've seen teachers now not trying to be perfect. They're more at ease. This helps emotionally and mentally."*

When asked about this time for students, compared with 9/11, Mr. Campbell provided a reflective answer, *"The first thing is social-emotional. This really affects our students. 9/11 was one event. This is different in that students will be remembering a time period. A positive part of it is being close to their families. Or maybe they might think they are trapped with their families. Might be a good or a not so good memory. Seniors graduating are missing year-end activities. They'll be missing the friendships, the connections, I think there will be both an appreciation for everyone they spent time with but also a sense of loss for what they were working so hard for. Not sure how they overcome. With 9/11, that moment in time was a feeling of loss and insecurity. This is different as a period of time, not as a moment of time."*

Mr. Campbell had some advice for other schools going through a time of emergency remote learning. *"Find the opportunity in this situation. As schools, if we don't come out doing things differently, we fail. Find opportunities for how we do school. Rarely is there an opportunity to change things like we have now. Every independent school faces challenges with how much time we have. There's a packed-in schedule, and we're always trying to understand how to do more without cutting anything. This is a real opportunity to change what teaching and learning are in the 21st Century. We can make real priorities."*

He continued, *"It's time for thinking of what it really means to be an independent school learner. To think about how to make that change in instruction - what to cut. This can be as much of a reset as possible. This is a great chance to change schedules. It's been an introduction to what distance learning can look like and how we can give more opportunities to the different way schedules change day-to-day. Before we go back to normal, if we do not think of all the ways we did things differently, we will have failed as educators. Find the opportunity to tip the reset. We can't go back to how things happened before. It's not a time to go back in the fall like every fall. We need to see this as an opportunity to prove why there is value in independent schools. To consider why school matters."*

Jason Curtis
Director of Technology and Associate Head of School
Thaden School, Bentonville AR

Thaden School moved quickly to online learning. Mr. Curtis shared, *"It was a good transition to online learning. Teachers were keeping relationships strong with their students. Good pedagogy translates to good relationships. Teachers worked to maintain those connections."*

Online learning meant connectivity at home. Conversations ensued to find out who already had Internet access, and who needed it. *"I think challenges we face right now tend to stem from how to ensure all of our students have solid connectivity to the Internet. Students don't need to be subsidized if parents don't need it. It becomes a tricky topic. We've been doing ad hoc one-off conversations with the kids to determine the need for connectivity. We passed out some cell hot spots if there's no Internet whatsoever."*

When asked what might be different in students' lives, Mr. Curtis replied, *"We are all locked down with our families. We are starting to connect in ways we haven't before. Kids are tired of being on cell phones - who thought that? Families are playing board games together, hiking in the creek together. If this crisis had not happened, this wouldn't have happened."*

Mr. Curtis explained, *"I'm hoping these connections last, and students yearn for these connections. I hope they still find time for each other. Work from home is happening, but in a compressed timeline and things still got done. People started wondering, 'Why have I been working so hard?' No need to pour your entire life into work. This crisis showed us something different."*

As to what would Mr. Curtis would tell other schools now going through this extraordinary time, he said, *"My advice is to lean into and embrace the change and see what you can learn from this. Everything is an opportunity to learn and grow. Explore fascinating new techniques, new things. Document what is going on now to transfer to the regular world when we go back."*

James Huffaker
Director of Technology
The Hun School, Princeton NJ

Asking about success stories from the COVID-19 crisis, Mr. Huffaker pointed immediately to leadership. He said, *"I think the way our Upper School and Middle School heads have handled the process of moving online might be a model on how to do it. They modified schedules and went right into formal training while being very supportive. They were doing what needed to be done to support the faculty."* He described how they leveraged school expertise, calling on *"education technology support and the IT dept and various faculty who had video conferencing for flipped classroom activities in the past."* The Hun School had resources already available.

"Having hardware resources in the hands of faculty and staff made transitioning that much easier not to worry about desktops."

As an American boarding/day school, there were challenges when the physical campus had to shut down and rely on remote learning. *"The biggest challenge has been keeping students attentive. I'm a senior advisor this year - the seniors have already checked out. They are upset that they will lose the traditions of graduations and fun of being that senior during the end of the school year."*

As an international school with students across the world, unique challenges occurred. How could a school provide the education parents had paid for when the delivery was suddenly through remote learning? Not every country has the same access to the Internet. Mr. Huffaker explained, *"Some students in Panama couldn't connect because of technology issues. Chinese students trying to access through VPNs are being are cut off."*

Considering what this meant for students currently and in the future, who have gone through this kind of school closing crisis, Mr. Huffaker identified areas of concern. *"Relationships. Personal and communal. It was magnified on a community scale. Kids are social animals, and we are humans looking for companionship. It has all been affected moving down the road. Even if this clears itself and we go back to some normalcy, it won't be complete."*

Mr. Huffaker points to shifts that have already occurred and talked of his 25-year old son. *"For kids, online dating IS already the norm and now even more so. I can't imagine what this all means for the next 20 years. Professionally, my son Alex is User Experience designing. Whenever I talk to him as a 25-year-old virtual worker, it's already his norm working with clients. He's in front of a laptop. For him, it's not a big impact on his professional life."*

He continued talking about students, *"Students have taken the art of communicating to a whole other level. There were bad players on Zoom that tried to disrupt our sessions. This generation has grown up with these bad actors. They see things all the time that we couldn't imagine seeing. Shocking things. It's a different world, and they've been living it for some time. It's the worry of the modern parent wanting to protect. These students live in this new world."*

Thinking of what advice Mr. Huffaker would offer to other schools, he said, *"Everyone has the same answer — we are all in it together. Education, as we know it with brick and mortar, has been turned on its ear. There's an expectation that you can't come in because you are sick. The expectation now is the virtual classroom. How do you affect the overall school as a place you want to be on a daily basis? This is changing fundamental traditional ways Americans have been taught."*

Vincent Jansen
Director of Technology
Southpointe Academy, Tsawwassen, British Columbia, Canada

Mr. Jansen cited parents in his success stories. *"Parents have been very supportive. There's a portal for parents in middle school, upper school, and junior school. Teachers have been loading condensed versions of information as a handout our parents can see and follow. We include parents as partners in education. As an administrator, I have IT coffee chats two days week to hear concerns, pros, and cons, what's working. We do a lunch and learn and professional development. There's a lot of support for the teachers. There's a combination of information service strategies in a learning environment."*

Commenting on how students may be changed by living through this crisis, Mr. Jansen said, *"We are seeing students are more connected to each other through devices. They're connecting two or three times during the same session. They might be on a Zoom call, but they're already on Discord and also chat on phones at the same time."*

Students collaborate through these multiple channels, says Mr. Jansen, *"They coalesce as a group, discussing answers to quizzes, tests. Their peer grouping is stronger. They're discovering together."*

He continues, *"Graduates, seniors, I don't know. They are the ones that finish the year and are concerned about graduations. They still do AP exams, just that it's open* book. It's too early to tell what will happen for adults. The new normal is going to be different than the old one. Dr. Shimmi Kang https://www.drshimikang.com/[48] —a neuroscientist—talks about executive functioning skills. Adaptability is the word she uses. People who are successful will adapt. For all of us. Kids are adapting all the time."

As to what he might say to other schools going through an extraordinary time, Mr. Jansen replies, "My key thing is lower your expectations of technology. Understand that people are not working from home. People are at home, during a crisis, trying to work. I've tried to emphasize that."

Mr. Jansen elaborates, "It's more challenging than now. Everyone is stressed out. I don't feel stressed out. Nothing will happen if something doesn't happen. Students and teachers need to know adaptability and reduce the anxiety. Don't rush. All of us do too much. Just relax, it will be fine. Relax."

Larry Kahn
Chief Technology Officer
Trinity Valley School, Fort Worth TX

Mr. Kahn shared how to find stories from Trinity Valley School during COVID-19, "Go to #trojansunited to see some success stories from making masks to really neat things for students. Teachers are sharing success stories themselves."

It's not just teachers and students reporting success, Mr. Kahn said, "It took the coronavirus for the technology department to get much-needed love from the Board of Directors and everyone else." In the four years that Mr. Kahn has been at Trinity Valley, he accomplished a lot that has now paid off during this crisis. He said, "Year one we gave teachers laptops. We really improved the iPad program and MDM. We got great control over that. We improved our Canvas LMS. All of those things lifted us when terrible things happened."

---

48 Drshimikang.com. n.d. accessed September 14, 2020.

Speaking of challenges during a global crisis that has caused the loss of life, jobs, and income Mr. Kahn said, *"What is suffering is equity. Some people may lose their relatives. Others will not. Some families will lose jobs or income; some will not."*

As to what might be different now and in the future for students, Mr. Kahn replied, *"I'm thinking of their relationship with parents. The screen time debate has gone away. We don't know the new normal for us, the world after this. I'm hoping that it will be positive. I researched articles about life after the Black Plague, the Spanish Flu, and culturally and economically life was better. The roaring 20s happened after the Spanish Flu. People will say, "Remember when school went online." One of the things we talked about – the fact that graduating seniors were born during 9/11. Most of them don't remember 9/11. They don't remember the 2008 financial crisis. This COVID-19 crisis they will remember the rest of their lives. We need to make schools as wonderful as possible."*

As to advice for other schools, Mr. Kahn shared, "Think of creative ways to embrace this opportunity."

Jason Kern
Assistant Head of School for Innovation and Learning
All Saints Episcopal School, Tyler TX

When you're with an experiential school with authentic hands-on learning and student agency as a unifying philosophy, aspects of authentic learning continue when the buildings are closed. Mr. Kern said, *"We're using 3D printers to make PPE to be sent all over the U.S. to alums and other people who are friends of the community. I hate that our kids can't be on campus to help in the process. Some students have taken home 3D printers. We have our own student-run ad agency and are working with schools in Atlanta and Maine to do this work. Our engineering kids are making simple machines and different concepts at home. We have fabrication kids. They're using tools at home."*

Continuing to describe learning from home during this crisis, Mr. Kern said, *"Every family has a different desire for learning. That's why we offer things in tiers. We break down a number of concepts so that you learn the concept. Here is the minimum just for the concept. What are the main pieces of the concept? We use videos to teach this. Then we move to extension exercises. We work on how to utilize pedagogy to have minimum concepts to learn. We give high ceiling projects."*

Mr. Kern described how All Saints Episcopal framed this unusual time. He said, *"It was triage – not remote learning. We were fortunate that it was the end of the school year. We'd already built relationships. We were using our face and our voice to connect with our learners. Most teachers were making weekly videos, having weekly connections with our students, meeting with students 1-on-1. We were trying to take advantage of not having to be constrained by schedule. We were not meeting simply by class."*

Consolidating concepts is a goal at All Saints Episcopal. Mr. Kern explained, *"We try to take advantage of not having to be constrained by schedule. We don't structure learning simply by class. If there are three sections of algebra, break into a Zoom on one Algebra concept. If you have that concept down, don't come to the Zoom. Rather than having arbitrary attendance in every class, we moved to just in time help."*

When asked about what students might think now and, in the future, going through a crisis and school closing, Mr. Kern said, *"These students will realize that community is more than physical. Being together is one sort of community, but an emotional community coming together does not have to be face-to-face. I hope they will walk away with an understanding of the regard their school and teachers have for them."*

Learning remotely will have an impact on students, said Mr. Kern, *"As a student who grew up playing travel baseball, I would take 4 to 6 weeks off from school, and when I returned I would realize what we did in school I could do in one-third of the time at home. I'd come back a week or two ahead."*

Mr. Kern continued, *"Students will have a different view on learning and school and that they can learn anywhere. They will have an appreciation for each other and what we do together."* He thinks they will understand the concept that

"You can work from anywhere and learn from anywhere. This will continue with this generation."

Thinking about what might be next for school in general, Mr. Kern says, *"We know from this experience that we need to have the ability to pedagogically switch between learning modalities. We have to take advantage of opportunities and know that teaching is not just face-to-face interactions. We need to know how to utilize technology when together and also when apart."*

Thinking about school in general, Mr. Kern shared, *"The biggest thing is we don't know how parents are going to deal if we can't get together. School is more than learning - it's community. It's time to have separation from parents and having different people influencing your child and helping mold your child. Independent school relies on a parent-school partnership. We have truly thought about how to support each other to create learners in the world."*

Advice for other schools going through a crisis from Mr. Kern was, *"Every school community is different. Understand your school community. Understand the needs they have, and expectations of what school offers them. A highly competitive Exeter type school has different expectations than an experiential school like Colorado Mountain School. Generalizing is dangerous. Use best practices. Aim for how to promote, enhance, and further your mission without trying to replicate what another school is doing. We are all different. How do you leverage the community and learning environment in the best way possible? Don't just say, 'this works great in Northern California' and try to use it in East Texas."*

Darryl Loy
Director of Modern Learning
Good Shepherd Episcopal School, Dallas TX

Mr. Loy described Good Shepherd's approach while the school was closed during the pandemic crisis. *"We are trying to maintain some kind of normalcy. There's daily communication between teacher and class in the Lower School. Middle School is on a 6-day rotation, so maybe not every day will see every teacher communicating with every student."*

He continued, *"We are focused on what we have remaining in terms of content mastery. The end of the year is more on reinforcement, less on the introduction of new concepts. We've pared down to focus on mastery. Because of that, we're making a shift to the content piece, and more synchronous instruction for check-ins see how kids are doing."*

When asked about success stories, Mr. Loy shared, *"One big one. My department has a design thinking specialist and education technologist giddy with the fact that every teacher is using technology, even the holdouts, and they are doing well. That's the biggest success story for us. Technology is on the main stage. How long have we been trying to get this?"*

Thinking about challenges, Mr. Loy described, *"A lot of our teachers who were less tech-savvy had to learn new software in some instances. None of the teachers knew Zoom before this. They had to step up and learn how to manage. We are using LMSs in ways we had not used before. We're using more cloud storage. We've been moving quickly from saving to servers to saving on Google drive. Virtually this happened in the first week."*

As to what students are going through, Mr. Loy said, *"Our hope is that students are stretched a bit from an educational perspective into taking ownership of their learning. They are becoming more of a self-advocate for their learning. They're maintaining a connection with their teachers. We hope they are embracing new ways to learn."*

He continued, *"But the downside is they are missing so many social aspects of their day to day class experiences interacting such as formal events, parties, graduation. Those events are not going to happen. We're still working through this and deciding how to address this, but some of it is lost. We will stick with kids."*

Mr. Loy offered some advice to other schools. *"The biggest thing is to really offer an abundance of grace and flexibility to faculty, students, and parents because it is an unprecedented time in our lives. There's no way to know what every student and family is going through. We have to extend that grace. It's okay. It's part of why we are switching from asynchronous to synchronous learning. Kids could have a sick parent at home. A lot of our families have both parents who are doctors. We extend grace to those families."*

Jason Ramsden
Chief Information Officer
Ravenscroft School, Raleigh NC

Mr. Ramsden described success stories while his school was closed due to the coronavirus. *"The biggest Aha! moment is we were concerned about how teachers would leverage distance learning (we are not calling it online.) It was all brand new to us, and we wondered if teachers would rise to this occasion and how this would all work. Success!"*

He elaborated, *"Purposely for the nine years previous, we had slowly moved everything to the cloud, went 1:1 with Chromebooks, and launched Google for Education. All before a precedent to react quickly. We found some things that worked during this distance learning, added some other software to our tool belt, and then we ran with it quickly. Biggest successes from this process: faculty were more prepared to do distance learning than we imagined – they rose to the occasion."*

Reflecting on parents at Ravenscroft, Mr. Ramsden shared, *"I think our parents have always appreciated our faculty for the time and effort they put into teaching their children but parents having been at home with kids and seeing teachers rise to this occasion has elevated how parents view our teachers. They really know they are rock stars. Our teachers take the time, effort, and make it seamless. They're not flying by the seat of their pants. Faculty has risen to the challenge. Lots of teachers put in a regular school day and don't always feel love. Now they're getting this back tenfold."*

When asked what might be different for students living through the extraordinary school closing because of coronavirus, Mr. Ramsden said, *"For this group of kids especially seniors, and for kids in college, they will be resilient moving forward. We've been teaching students how to be resilient here at Ravenscroft as part of our Lead From Here citizen leader program, but these kids will be incredibly resilient and able to handle tough situations rather than kids that didn't go through this. This provided real examples of handling disappointment - incredible disappointment. The level of disappointment and handling this in the future will make them stronger, and they will see life differently."*

Mr. Ramsden offered some advice to other schools: *"At least for independent schools, ATLIS (Association of Technology Leaders in Independent School) have been able to rally independent school communities and weekly town hall meetings. Just the coming together of everybody. Pulling people together. Pulling people together to have this commonality that we are all in this together, and we will come out the other side better."*

He continued, *"For technology directors, this has elevated our roles in the eyes of heads and business administrators. Before we worked in the shadows. Leaders will understand how important it is to have someone leading technology in schools."*

William Stites
Director of Technology
Montclair Kimberley Academy, Montclair NJ

Mr. Stites shared how Montclair Kimberly Academy reacted to emergency remote learning because of COVID-19 which happened near spring break. *"We already had an internal task force composed of school administrators and educators. They created a nitty-gritty plan, but we still needed to get the word out to the school. Years ago, we had a plan for what school would look like for extended closure. It was a plan for a week or so, nothing like now. This time it's for months. We adapted and extended that plan."*

Mr. Stites was concerned with cybersecurity and privacy. *"These issues expanded once all devices were in students' and teachers' homes using their own Internet access. How was learning to happen synchronously via video conferencing?"*

Guidelines were developed, infused with the mission and philosophy of MKA. Mr. Stites shared, *"We always had an open-door policy. The teacher was never behind a closed door. There would always be a clear view of everyone."* Moving to video conferencing included *"recording so that everything is at least captured. We set some norms up as to what it looks like. We decided how students raise their hands, how students are dressed, when to mute the video, when you can take a screenshot, all of these things."*

When asked what advice he would share with other schools, Mr. Stites replied, *"Stick to what you know and limit the new. This is not a time to be jumping in and trying things for the first time and hoping it will go. You can later expand."*

Mr. Stites continued, *"Build the core around the foundation, around what is tested, vetted, and known, and what professional development you've already done. Anxiety is ratcheted up. People are anxious to get things right. Everyone becomes eager for more structure, the things that school provides. It's not about what's new, not during a crisis."*

Catholic School Interviews

Tara Johanneson
Technology Integrationist and Teacher
Bishop O'Gorman Catholic Schools, Sioux Falls SD

Ms. Johanneson was asked about success stories and right away thought of teachers. She said, *"Teachers were very prepared and ready to make the leap quickly."*

A shift was occurring. Mr. Johanneson continued. *"There were some holdouts and some who struggled more. Some teachers were not as tech-savvy. We're working on bringing them up to speed. It's very positive for schools — teachers are going to be more technology advanced or just comfortable using technology in the classroom. Teachers see technology not as a device but as a way to extend learning. Ultimately, that's why we use technology in the classroom. The separation between it's a device and how do I use it."*

Moving to challenges, Ms. Johanneson described the experience at Bishop O'Gorman around assumptions, *"One of the things teachers were most unprepared for was the lack of skills our kids have. Overall, teachers thought students would be very proficient. Instead, students lacked the skills needed to be successful in a virtual classroom - not just the focus and drive, but technology competencies have been spoon-fed to them. Another thing hard for everyone was parents were not aware of what was happening and didn't know the tools, products, and devices. Some do know the tools. Some don't. Some struggle."*

Thinking of what might be different to students going through a crisis, Ms. Johanneson shared, *"I primarily teach seniors. It impacted them a lot. My students do a daily journal. They talk a lot about how they are feeling and their overall mental state because of what is going on and what is being canceled. I really think that we cannot take anything for granted."*

She continued, *"It's such a jolt to the system, especially for the senior class. They feel robbed of so many things. It feels like wear and tear to go to school every day, but they would give anything to go back to school. They are so disappointed. Thank goodness I get to go to work today. People are drowning in so much grief. Everyone in general. So many don't get to go to work right now."*

Reflecting on what advice Ms. Johanneson would have for other schools, she said, *"Less is more. Everyone has said that. I'm reading student journals and seeing my own children go through this as well. Everyone is trying to address standards and fill this time in school. That's not what this is about."*

Elaborating on remote learning, she said, *"Giving them something to do to prevent total regression or slide but planning to fill seven hours of work is not the right answer. We don't study for seven hours, we move, we have lunch, and we transfer knowledge from each other. School isn't seven hours of looking at a computer and doing homework. The last thing we want to do is make them hate school. This could very well be a side effect of this."*

She continued, *"This is also a great opportunity to take content and apply it to what is happening in the real world to make correlations. Explore how content is relevant to the outside. Build a fort in the backyard, bake a recipe. There are so many ways to teach content at home."*

Milena Streen
VP and Chief Information Officer
St. Ignatius High School, Cleveland OH

Ms. Streen described the process once the COVID-19 crisis hit. *"We found out we would be closed on Thursday but luckily had a professional development day already scheduled Friday. That started the process. Friday, we had teachers in, and Monday and then Tuesday was St Patrick's Day, so the boys—St. Ignatius is an all-boys schoo—had the day off. Instruction began on March 18. We had to pivot quickly. We had to look for a teaching platform. We bought Zoom licenses for teachers and staff through the Ohio consortium. Technology engineers trained on Zoom and made a checklist of what to cover. Teachers worked one-on-one with technology engineers. They did a good job of making teachers comfortable. We were already using G Suite and were very comfortable with that."*

She continued, *"We took a lot of computers out of the library. We gave them to kids who needed a device. We gave out hotspots as well. The need was mostly the younger students who didn't have a computer. Sometimes Wi-Fi is spotty with so many people using their internet at home. The hot spots boosted coverage for overloaded Wi-Fi."*

Ms. Streen had success stories to share. *"I couldn't be prouder of our school. When we started school on Wednesday, we were just overwhelmed. Everyone figured it out. All faculty, all staff, everyone came together. We had a chance to talk and share. A lot of teachers are doing incredible things. Teachers are doing a phenomenal job of checking in. Teachers reported the existing multicultural students' group with their staff advisors was still meeting. We have not left students behind. We wrapped our campus ministry in ."*

Ms. Streen continued, *"Some students were not engaged. We've been calling parents who were saying, 'We need help.' Athletic trainers have been doing Zoom yoga. The Zoom yoga classes are for students and parents. Attendance has been amazing. There's a sense of community. It's not just academics. We're broadcasting the daily Mass. Students could take five minutes to stop and reflect on the day. There's a sense of consistency even though we're not on campus."*

As to challenges, Ms. Streen shared, *"You need to change the mindset when there's no face-to-face instruction. You can't expect teachers to mimic the same school day. It's not realistic. Those challenges are around getting teachers to flip their mindset and their level of expectations. That was really one of the hardest things because, at first, there was resistance. Then once they started teaching virtually, it became a much different animal than every day. We had a detailed end of the year procedure."*

With this crisis interrupting school, Ms. Streen reflected on what this meant to students. *"Oh my gosh! Seniors were devastated. There are so many rituals that accompany the end of the year. St. Ignatius students looked forward to freshman baccalaureate Mass, graduation, prom, and retreat trips. All of these things were canceled, and we can't be sure if they will ever get them back. We postponed graduation and did not make it virtual. Students want to go through everything as best as they can. We are sending care packages, graduation things for their yards."*

Ms. Streen added, *"This generation will feel like they missed something. They missed that journey. You think of your high school graduation as a feeling of moving on. I'm not sure these students will even move to college campuses. That's the hard thing. But I think that they will realize that there's not much but to get through this. There will be resilience."*

Thinking of advice to other schools going through an emergency learning crisis, Ms. Streen offered, *"I would think that number one would be patience. Number* two would be that students have to be engaged across multiple areas in terms of communication. Communication needs to happen—up, down, across—talking to teachers and parents. Even if you don't know everything right now, communicating is a good thing rather than just leaving people in limbo. Expectations have changed, and what might have been perfect isn't the same. Show up to work on time and put in eight hours. Think that there could be kids sitting on teachers' laps. Our same employees are also daycare providers teaching their own children while helping students. You have to be cognizant of what employees are going through. Expectations have to be adjusted."

International School Interviews

Warren Apel
Director of Technology
The American School in Japan, Tokyo, Japan

Japan is right for a distance learning plan, according to Warren Apel. *"We could have an earthquake any day."* The American School in Japan acted quickly, having heard from colleagues at schools in China and Hong Kong who had already begun closing. ASIJ updated their existing closure plans and aligned them to their current vision of learning. They began distance learning with two days of professional development for teachers. On the last day of in-person classes, they made sure students took their laptops, iPads, and chargers home. Mr. Apel says, *"In my entire career in ed-tech, I've never had such a strong turnout to a voluntary technology training. People were ripe to learn."* Part of the two days of planning and professional development included workshops on screencasting, video conferencing, and using appointment slots for booking video calls on Google Calendar. Teachers also learned ways to communicate, assess, and provide feedback using FlipGrid, EdPuzzle, Padlet, Quizziz, and HyperDocs. *"We had planned for the distance learning to last two weeks, so we knew it had to be meaningful learning. We weren't just going to send home a few days' worth of worksheets."*

The challenges of an international school existed. *"At first, we had no idea what time zone kids would be in – would they flee to America, stay in Tokyo apartments? If they were to go to Thailand to wait it out, they might not have good Wi-Fi."*

Mr. Apel is proud of how teachers rose to the challenge, *"I'm proud of how we kept the learning alive. Teachers worked harder than ever, staying up late. It was stressful. The community was coming together. We adjusted the schedule and refined it each week. We adjusted the balance between synchronous and asynchronous lessons and added time for teachers and teams to meet and plan. There was a high level of collaboration."* Many employees who weren't front line teachers pitched in. *"Playground supervisors in elementary school had no children to supervise, so they helped to make videos with teachers in the elementary school."*

Like other educators interviewed, Mr. Apel puts social-emotional concerns front and center. *"Most of our challenges were social-emotional; teachers are stressed out. Many have their own children at home, doing distance learning themselves."* The American School in Japan was proud of its data dashboard they created based on surveys of teachers, students, and parents. They triangulated the data to get a real picture of how their stakeholders were feeling. They could drill down and find out which parents were saying there was high stress in their family, and which parents said they were doing well. Counselors could see how much sleep students were getting. It also allowed ASIJ to track where students were physically, including their time zone. The school could know how many students would be available at 8:30 a.m. in Tokyo, for instance. This information helped with adjusting the balance between synchronous and asynchronous class meetings.

Using education technology alongside face-to-face instruction had always been an option. But with a remote distance learning plan that relied on video and other tools, faculty had to jump in to use more technology than ever. Teachers rose to that challenge.

The tech department had to support more than just students and teachers; they had to move to remote support, which included helping students in their homes. Apel said that before the COVID-19 crisis, *"… our ticketing system was mostly used by teachers. Students would go in person to the tech assistant in school if they needed help. They walked down the hall to get help in person. And they could also send an email. Every now and then, I would get an email from a parent. Those parent emails were not frequent. Once we started distance learning, a major ramp up on tech support requests ensued."*

To the question, "What would you tell other schools now going through this kind of extraordinary time?" Mr. Apel replied, *"This was an opportunity to focus on what learning is really important. We emphasized to teachers that less is more, and to maximize student time. What are the essential outcomes now? We wanted meaningful learning. You can't change every teacher's pedagogical process overnight. If we can't do tests and lectures the way we always did, and we know that learning is social and personal, maybe right now is a once-in-a-lifetime opportunity to think outside the box and do things differently. We can give teachers permission to try something new and really maximize learning in a way that makes the best of the situation."*

Students shared their experiences in a podcast

When Mr. Apel was asked about what students experienced and thought about their future, he cited, "What's the Dealio," a podcast that was created by the students at the American School in Japan. One episode focused on what students were thinking about as they lived through this extraordinary time. They had to quickly leave school and not return during the school year or, for some, not return again. This student podcast episode is especially relevant – the word "resilient" was used by the students to describe their own experiences when everything in school was upended:

https://podcasts.apple.com/us/podcast/whats-the-dealio/id147848907849

---

49 Apple Podcasts. What's the Dealio. *2019-20: Year in Review.* June 9, 2020. accessed September 3, 2020.

Burcu Aybat
Primary and Middle School Principal
Ielev School, Istanbul, Turkey

Ms. Aybat reported that Turkey had a national educational platform to help teachers with remote and online learning. The system included an LMS (Learning Management System) with resources and opportunities for discussions and collaboration. Having this platform eased all schools in Turkey into remote learning, with many teachers familiar with the tools.

Ms. Aybat's school had many tech-savvy teachers; Ielev is an Apple Distinguished school. Ms. Aybat has authored several education technology books focused on teachers, so she provided strong leadership.

Instruction was delivered both asynchronously and synchronously. Ms. Aybat said, *"Setting up routines was very important. We tried to balance synch and async."*

Teachers worked collaboratively, sometimes led by the school's Apple Distinguished Educators. She reported they gave classroom examples and encouraged one another. There was a *"… kind of natural leadership that happened. We gave a lot of training sessions to teach pedagogical strategies. Teacher training and morale and motivation are important,"* said Ms. Aybat.

Like other leaders interviewed, Ms. Aybat was concerned with the social-emotional health of teachers and students. She reported that it's essential to look at the *"lack of separate home life and school life. We cannot now separate this. This is an emergency situation, not planned online learning. We explained to teachers that it is not online learning. It's emergency online learning."*

Ielev School surveyed parents after the first week of online learning and then two times later. The first survey score was 74 but moved up to 83 in a later survey. The perception was that it was going well and that parents were listening, reported Ms. Aybat.

When asked about challenges, Ms. Aybat said, *"Teacher motivation, morale. Parents are too involved in the process. School needs to lead the teaching. There needs to be close communication with parents and institutional communication between parents and schools."*

To help with communication, Ielev provided *"… one channel where parents can get true information."* Ms. Aybat recommended, *"Create a good communication channel."* Video conferencing was challenging and took longer than face-to-face meetings, so they found having too many Zoom meetings was not productive.

Another challenge Ms. Aybat identified is Assessment. Assessment is different when using emergency remote learning. She said, *"Teachers are doing classes online and synchronously, but how do you assess them?"* They used *"… formative assessment tools and small tests at the end of class."* Standardized tests and national scores presented another challenge. *"We have objectives. An academy excellence vision is in our mission statement. We have a standardized test. A complication is the online test platform."*

When asked about students' lives during and after the COVID-19 pandemic, Ms. Aybat replied, *"Students will learn on Zoom or Internet - students will wonder what the reason that I will be in school? Schools should offer them what cannot be offered online. Students are mostly meeting their friends, teachers, and being together and socializing. They need a reason to go to school."* It becomes an opportunity for educators to ponder how a school is effective or not. Ms. Aybat continued, "Put ourselves in the innovation process. Think about school benefits. Everything has changed. "

When asked what she'd say to other schools going through emergency learning, she said, *"It's teamwork. Communication is so important. Not quantity, but quality is important. The teacher is the key. Every school has its own story."*

Mario Fishery
Director of Technology Support
American School of Bombay, Mumbai, India

The American School of Bombay in India operated several task forces to support their school community during this global pandemic:

- Research and Development
- Virtual Learning 2.0
- Faculty and Staff
- Health and Wellness
- Start of School
- Parent Education
- Communications
- Schedules and Layouts
- Support Services

ASB actually practiced what would happen if schools closed down. Their previous experience with SARS involved two weeks of being shut down, but COVID-19 closed the school for a longer period of time.

Social-emotional health was front and center, and ASB surveyed the community. Mr. Fishery says, *"We sent out regular surveys, and were rated very high during virtual learning. Students connected with teachers, engaged with content."* To help the community stay in touch, The American School in Bombay set up regular online parent cafés for their elementary, middle, and high schools. ASB also set up a single landing page for communication and video tutorials on their EdTech channel for virtual learning. They reported high levels of engagement between students, parents, faculty, and staff. School psychologists advised students, listened to what they were going through, what they needed to do, and even provided lessons on how to securely save electronic files.

When asked about challenges, Mr. Fishery mentioned faculty at an international school who had previously resided elsewhere. *"We had teachers check out devices to use for virtual learning. Teachers were also provided support if they wanted to move back to their home country. Those teachers who left for their home countries were given a two- or three-day break, to get set up and have Internet connections. Moving the staff was challenging."*

For students who needed laptops and technology equipment, logistics were complex. Mumbai was on lockdown, and it wasn't easy to get out to check out a device. The school had to make special provisions to provide support to the families that needed help.

ASB has many working parents, so the staff wanted to be sure the lessons were easy for the parents to help implement. In the elementary school, there was more of a partnership with parents, but middle school and older students were more independent. Still, if a child didn't respond when a teacher attempted to reach out, ASB would email the parents to check and see if any support was required.

Attendance became an issue. Teachers and students scattered to all corners of the world during this pandemic. ASB created groups of teachers and found ways to connect with parents of students who were not responding or keeping current.

Speaking about students going through an extraordinary time with schools closed, Mr. Fishery mentioned seniors and how graduation would not be the same, and how difficult it might be for children to sign yearbooks and receive year-end recognition. This was all managed online, and ASB successfully hosted live virtual graduation recognition ceremonies, assemblies, board meetings, and town hall meetings.

For elementary students, Mr. Fishery said, *"It's not easy for them to be confined to home over a period of time, and the school provided some amazing videos and content to stay engaged and fit. (The physical education team created some awesome videos hosted on ASB's ed-tech channel.) Middle school and high school are always part of this digital world. Being told to go out and play, that's a little tough for them. How are kids going to grow up? Only time will tell."*

ASB made sure students could reach out. Mr. Fishery described, *"We counseled kids. Our counseling office was always open; students could have a virtual session."*

As for advice to other schools going through this extraordinary time, Mr. Fishery shared,

"Don't try to replicate what you do on a regular school day. If we were just starting online now, we would connect with the kids in a way that you have sessions to get engaged, then build up to an online presence. Start with that. Don't start with assignments, exams. Have a time when they can connect with you virtually. Kids always want to see their teachers and classmates. Synchronous time to connect helps. Have a good, blended program of synchronous and asynchronous sessions."

He added, *"Everyone was all around the world, and synchronous meetings were set up for the India time zone, making sessions available to students who were across different time zones. However, with the staff being placed in different time zones, teachers were not always able to have synchronous sessions with students outside the India time zone. The online program became more personalized. We found where kids and parents were located and what time zone and came up with plans. A lot of kids were sleeping and getting up later. Kids ages twelve to fifteen need a lot of sleep, and they were getting more sleep during the school closure."*

Mr. Fishery continued, *"Teachers needed to upgrade their online skills and get tech-savvy with technology. Those who were not so comfortable with technology were provided with a support structure by the tech and ed-tech department to upgrade their skills. We have a GREAT technology department to support teachers and the ASB community. The IT Helpdesk runs a virtual help desk from 7:30 am - 10:00 pm to support the entire community. Community support is vital. Everyone should be able to ask people for help."*

Dan Hudkins
Chief Information Officer
Taipei American School, Taipei City, Taiwan

Mr. Hudkins and his team had shored up Taipei American School over time, implementing SSO (Single Sign-On) solutions on Azure cloud servers, a whole school LMS since 2017, 1-to-1 for grades 6-12, and SeeSaw for PreK-5th grade. This helped them with the crisis from COVID-19, although they were only closed for three weeks following the Chinese New Year and one additional week in April following spring break.

Still, those three weeks required planning, collaboration, and rethinking of the schedule. They were not sure how long the school would be closed.

Mr. Hudkins shared regarding the middle school, *"We were on a relatively conventional eight period day. That doesn't work with online learning. A group of teachers got together to focus on core classes and considered what it meant with less frequent meetings."* Mr. Hudkins explained that *"A lot of coordination needs to happen when the usual schedule is not followed, especially in middle and high school with multiple teachers and subjects involved."*

Thinking of the different divisions involved, Mr. Hudkins said, *"Lower was the most successful, the one about which I was most worried, but the best. They had already built a home/school connection in SeeSaw. And the ratio of education technology teachers to teachers is higher than in other divisions. The campus was open, and there could be physical meetings. Teachers could do a lot of team planning and reflection."*

Mr. Hudkins described how school changed at Taipei American School. *"We are wearing all masks all the time. The country said 1.5 meters apart or wear a mask. We are doing all masks. We have tents to spread people apart at mealtimes, and cafeteria seating is limited. It's a tropical country, so we can do this. Classes have been conducted as usual."*

It's essential that school administrators provided leadership and continuity. Mr. Hudkins said, *"The only thing radically different is all administration meetings are on Zoom because we don't want one sick administrator making all the administrators sick."*

Other adults are also a concern. Mr. Hudkins shared, *"The faculty meeting is not a hands-on meeting. There is no large group meeting of faculty. Parents only come to school by appointment. Anyone who is not staff or a student and wants to visit fills out a form re: travel in the last fourteen days. We also do fever checking."*

Like most schools, there was a local or national governing body with recommendations. Mr. Hudkins reported, *"Following the Taiwan Ministry of Education, if you have a student who is quarantined and diagnosed positive, you have to close all the classes that student was in. If two students tested positive, you probably have to close the school."*

When asked what living through the COVID-19 crisis might mean for students and their future, Mr. Hudkins responded, *"This whole cohort of students will approach the question of online collaboration with a depth of comfort like never before. Kids going through this will not have a skew towards bricks and mortar as inherently better. The rest of the world will think bricks and mortar are better."*

As to faculty who have gone through this crisis, Mr. Hudkins speculated, *"One of the things that will be different even next year will be our faculty is much more conscious of how to use online tools to better know students who are introverted or less quick as well as the quick and bright students."* Mr. Hudkins recommended an approach to let students learn by hearing them and not speaking as often. He explains, *"'Shut up and start talking' is how you should teach with discussion boards in an online class. Let the online tools help teachers hear every student's voice. Teachers will integrate more online instruction into their classrooms."*

Mr. Hudkins offered advice to other schools, saying, *"Be prepared for how to come back. We are the only school that came back so far. How are you going to gather your data, so you know what you will do next time? Who is responsible? Who keeps the data up? In the international world, it's in the water to adapt to closings like this."* Hudkins further recommended designating a small team to determine *"... this is how we are coming back; this is how we are helping faculty to recover; this is how we are helping students to recover."*

Product Manager/Board of Education member

Leo Brehm
Product Manager at Catch On
Lifelong IT director in Massachusetts
Member of the Local School Board of Education

Mr. Brehm described experiences at his local public school, where he is on the board of education. He also shared his wife's experience as a public-school teacher, other school districts he follows, and what it was like to be a parent during the extraordinary time of remote emergency learning.

First, Mr. Brehm cited the importance of communication and described the downside when communication is not active and through. *"There's been some poor communication to staff, community. That leads to confusion, lots of questions. It causes morale issues. There needs to be more consistent support."*

Like most interviewees, he had praise for teachers. *"A lot of teachers are stepping up to change their practice, to do what's best for their practice. No one becomes a teacher for fame or money. Most are very dedicated to their craft and willing to try something if they believe it will meet students where they are."*

He worried about some students thrown into emergency remote learning. *"Immediately schools should focus on at-risk students. Engaged parents will have students succeed, but what about the at-risk population with two working parents, troubled or challenging situation at homes, single parents with multiple children and working while their kids are home."*

The equity issue was also a concern. "There should be equitable access to technology to engage in remote learning. There should be training of teachers for the delivery of remote instruction." This training includes acknowledging that not all remote learning is with technology. Mr. Brehm said remote instruction is different if not done with technology. He said remote learning without technology "… *is not as effective.*" Drawing from his own experience with virtual schools, Mr. Brehm said remote learning "… *could create flexibility and opportunities, but a truly virtual environment gives challenges to the social-emotional experience.*" This concern should be addressed.

Advice to other schools from Mr. Brehm included, "*Make sure students are fed, that they are getting the care they need at home, consider the touchpoints of school as a center of the community. Use Zoom, iChat. Email is not enough. Encourage communication between peers. Keep those relationships going. Students miss going to school. Social-emotional relationships are important. Have schools focus on maintaining connections. Connect any way you can. Ensure there is continuity of relationships with students, teachers, and the classroom. Believe in teachers and stand by them.*"

The Interview Questions

- What is being done at your school/district to address education with schools closed?
- Are there any success stories you'd like to share?
- Are there any overcoming challenges stories to share?
- How has the relationship between students and teachers adjusted?
- How has the relationship between parents and teachers adjusted?
- Are you supporting parents, teachers, students differently now?
- 9/11 changed things and a generation grew up in that shadow.
  - What/how do you think will change for students now and what might they remember/regret/embrace about how COVID changed things?
- What would you tell other schools now going through this extraordinary time?

Bibliography

Alliance for Excellent Education. Future Ready Schools. *Students of Color Caught in the Homework Gap*. https://futureready.org/homework-gap/?fbclid=IwAR1pTFJzwx8fnNV20uAQx16Ugfd1KrbR7XeXlLanEIY4K-jUuD1fPJTNPck. n.d. accessed September 14, 2020.

bakerSCCOE. LiveBinders. *Getting Remote Learning Right*. TICAL project. n.d. https://www.livebinders.com/b/2674057?fbclid=IwAR3TkXsJQCcMoDKqjocX9nU1G77y3ganHPbHdRIOGp_LQviYG8KV4_Z-eZo. accessed September 1, 2020.

Fleming, Nora. Edutopia. *Why are Some Kids Thriving During Remote Learning?* https://www.edutopia.org/article/why-are-some-kids-thriving-during-remote-learning?fbclid=IwAR3eHKejLSxHi-qCj1fhJrZDmIg_nNiIxmGwlaJ17iVIQ3aHoX9vatuaFbE. April 24, 2020. Accessed July 12, 2020.

Gonzalez, Jennifer. Cult of Pedagogy. *A 4-Part System for Getting to Know Your Students*. https://www.cultofpedagogy.com/relationship-building/. July 10, 2016. accessed August 3, 2020.

Gross, Natalie. EducationDive. *1:1 Programs 'On Steroids' Bring Challenges for School Districts*.https://www.educationdive.com/news/11-programs-on-steroids-bring-challenges-for-school-districts/584440/?utm_source=Sailthru&utm_medium=email&utm_campaign=Issue:%20 2020-09-01%20K-12%20Education%20Dive%20Newsletter%20

%5Bissue:29422%5D&utm_term=Education%20Dive:%20K12. n.d. accessed September 12, 2020.

Kamenetz, Anya. NPR NWPD. *What parents can learn from child care centers that stayed open during lockdowns.* https://www.npr.org/2020/06/24/882316641/what-parents-can-learn-from-child-care-centers-that-stayed-open-during-lockdowns. June 24, 2020. accessed September 1, 2020.

Molnar, Michele. EdWeek Market Brief. *Number of Ed-Tech Tools in Use Has Jumped 90 Percent Since School Closures.* https://marketbrief.edweek.org/marketplace-k-12/access-ed-tech-tools-jumped-90-percent-since-school-closures/?fbclid=IwAR3eHKejLSxHi-qCj1fhJrZDmIg_nNiIxmGwlaJ17iVIQ3aHoX9vatuaFbE. July 8, 2020. Accessed September 3, 2020.

NCLD.org. *Inclusive Technology during the COVID-19 Crisis.* www.ncld.org/covid19inclusivetech. July 2020. accessed September 12, 2020.

Natanson, Harrah. The Washington Post. *Love or hate them pandemic learning pods are here to stay – and could disrupt American education.* https://www.washingtonpost.com/local/education/love-or-hate-them-pandemic-learning-pods-are-here-to-stay--and-could-disrupt-american-education/2020/09/02/3d359f8c-dd6f-11ea-8051-d5f887d73381_story.html?fbclid=IwAR3eHKejLSxHi-qCj1fhJrZDmIg_nNiIxmGwlaJ17iVIQ3aHoX9vatuaFbE. September 2, 2020. Accessed September 5, 2020.

Reilly, Katie. TIME. *With No End in Sight to the Coronavirus, Some Teachers are Retiring Rather Than Going Back to School.* https://time.com/5864158/coronavirus-teachers-school/?fbclid=IwAR1AzbV-0maKcxEA3LZgzvPKk7xbbDdJoxNYlFDhPA_kPo0XAvtrHwUCG8A. July 8, 2020. accessed August 13, 2020.

Schroeder, Sarah, Jane, Rosemary. Edutopia. *How Using a Little Sign Language Can Improve Online Classes.* https://www.edutopia.org/article/how-using-little-sign-language-can-improve-online-class. September 14, 2020. Accessed September 14, 2020.

Schwartz, Sarah. Education Week. *It Was a Bumpy Ride, but Virtual Schooling During the Coronavirus Boosted Teachers' Tech Skills* https://www.edweek.org/ew/articles/2020/06/03/it-was-a-bumpy-ride-but-virtual.html . June 2, 2020. Accessed August 11, 2020.

Seltzer, Katie. Edutopia. *Engaging Students in Virtual Instruction With the Camera Off.* https://www.edutopia.org/article/engaging-students-virtual-instruction-camera. September 14, 2020. Accessed September 14, 2020.

Strauss, Valerie. The Washington Post. *Does homework work when kids are learning all day at home?* https://www.washingtonpost.com/education/2020/09/01/does-homework-work-when-kids-are-learning-all-day-home. September 1, 2020. accessed September 14, 2020.

Strauss, Valerie. The Washington Post. *Returning more kids to school is going to require a bolder plan.* https://www.washingtonpost.com/education/2020/09/11/returning-more-kids-school-is-going-require-bolder-plan/ September 11, 2020. accessed September 14, 2020.

Made in the USA
Middletown, DE
11 November 2020